TRUTH

TRIALS-TRIBULATIONS-INTEGRITY

I0152993

BY JOANNE CARTER

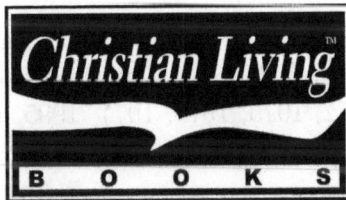

Christian Living™

B O O K S

Christian Living Books, Inc.
Largo, MD
We bring your dreams to fruition.

ISBN 978-1-56229-250-8

Christian Living Books, Inc.
P. O. Box 7584
Largo, MD 20792
ChristianLivingBooks.com

We bring your dreams to fruition.

Printed in the United States of America.

Contents

Acknowledgments

My precious Jesus Christ I give you praise. Much love and thanks to Jeanette Carter-Merritt, Sharon J. Cook, Mary Newman, Mary F. Morris and Regina Bunn for telling your truth.

Chapter 1

Navigating the Seasons of Life

If you have ever felt like praying something like this, you are not alone: "Lord, you know there is a devil that lives in me, I pray for her. Please God, don't let anyone make her come out to play." Life is a series of challenges and tests. It comes fully equipped with pleasure and pain, sunshine and rain. It is a potpourri of every fe eling imaginable. I have been in the storm, and I have stood by the ones I love in the storm. I must tell you – the storm does pass after a while. The thunder quits clapping, the rain stops, the clouds clear, and the morning breaks. What a blessing it is when the night has been so long, to know that at last it is morning.

I have held my head up through storms and night seasons. God knows, I am not a perfect person. I am a broken person who has held on to God. It is so nice to know, I did not have to stumble through life alone on crippled feet and twisted knees. I have decided to walk all the way, rain or shine, right or wrong, weak or strong. My past explains how I got here, my future determines where I'm headed.

I believe tests from God are structured to feed us. When you overcome a test or a storm, you should celebrate. If you are in a storm right now, know that it *will* pass over. Trouble doesn't last always. God is looking for people who will value their blessings. He has given us many victories. Don't devalue His blessings. Don't let your past pickpocket your future!

PLAYING THOSE SILLY GAMES

In my younger years, I thought that in order to have friends, I had to play their silly games. I soon realized that setting yourself up was not the best policy. I promise you, no devil in hell said you need anyone that much. Seek Jesus. He is the only One we need. The payback you get from Jesus is "NO CHARGE." When you place your problems in the master's hands, there is nothing too hard for Him. It's the worship in me that will penetrate throughout my surroundings into the hearts of others. We have to keep the Word of God moving.

I ask God to lead me, take my hand, guide me and teach me how to live the life He has planned for me. God said, "Look a little closer, the road is already paved for you." God has changed me with His undying love. He has set my soul free. I am not the girl I used to be. I gave my soul to God, and He gave me a brand new life. I will serve Him faithfully, for He is worthy.

Many years ago, I found myself sitting on the couch, holding my Bible tightly, wondering: "Why am I here? And for what purpose?" I looked around at all I had accomplished and asked myself, "Is *this* what life is about? Did I miss something?" I realized God had given me many talents. God gave me life so I could bring Him joy. He protects me, stands up for me, gave me a home and many blessings. I cannot express the peace and happiness I have today.

What do you do when you can no longer be the person you are? When you take a glance at your life now – where do you go from here? Why not live an inspiring life? Breathe in the life God chose for you. Get creative, try different things. Learn about things that are out of your league. Most of us talk about how to get ahead. So do something about it. Tap into that person who is hidden beneath the surface. Take a dare-devil escape into the wide blue yonder. Cleanse your mind; make it work a little overtime. You will see the world the way God sees it. Take a leap of faith. Get it right, keep it tight. Take the plunge. Stop waiting for God to get rid of the things we created. God gave us abilities to recognize our shortcomings. God did not create weapons, we did. Now we use them to wreak more havoc than the law allows. People, these are eye-opening moments! When you need to choose a weapon, choose the Bible.

LET GO AND WATCH GOD WORK

Keep God on your radar. He is your eyes and ears. God has always used others to deliver His blessings. Be careful not to gossip. The purpose of serving God is to love Him more than you love yourself. It's not hard at all. Just let Him fight your battles. Take a coffee break and watch Him work on your behalf. You know He is a miracle worker. So why not give Him the opportunity to set your mind free.

Your job is to get to a certain point. You have to put on your big boy/girl pants and be God's helper. Be patient, tolerant, kind, understanding, generous, peaceful, joyous, and loving. Does it sound like you are rendering a lot? Not at all; the benefits are much greater than you could ever imagine. Take the time to thank God as He clears obstacles and road blocks so that your walk with Him will be much smoother. God will always be there for you. Keep Him in front of you always.

You can do this! Do something to make your life just a little better and brighter. There is no other way to get to heaven. Make up your mind, let God know you are ready. Serve Him, worship Him and love Him with every fiber of your being.

SHARON'S STORY

My friendship with Sharon extends over thirty-four years. Over the years, we have talked about God often. One day, she asked me, "What is the definition of a friend?"

After asking that question, she referred to a definition of a friend given by the *Webster Dictionary, which says,* "person one knows well and likes." However, Sharon's own definition of a friend is someone who she can trust, depend on, and talk to about everything – someone who will be there for her through thick and thin.

"Wow!" she said, "I should have looked up *Webster's* definition and remembered there's not a friend like Jesus."

Sharon talked about her thirteen-year-old son taking her through the mill. He was destroying her home, not going to school and breaking into the house when he was supposed to be in school.

He would curse me out. He is what I call my problem child. His father and I separated in 2009 and things just got worse. It was always me against two – if you know what I mean. December of 2012, I wrote a letter to his father explaining how things were. Since I got no support from him, he needed to make arrangements to come and pick-up Jamaal because Jamaal wanted to be with him. In the back of my mind, I was thinking that once Jamaal was with his father, we would co-parent.

In response, his father picked him up. I assumed he was going to take Jamaal back to stay at his mother's house. But I was wrong. I found out through the grapevine that Jamaal was staying with his godmother who I thought was my friend – why else would she be his godmother?

I called his father to see what was going on and, of course, I had a million questions. He would never answer any of my calls. I called the godmother and her answer was that I needed to talk to his father.

My heart was already broken because I had no relationship with my son. Now, I had to face this mess. I cried many nights, I prayed to the Lord asking Him why, and I sang songs to help with the pain.

One morning, I woke up with the song, "What a Friend we have in Jesus." That song stayed with me all day. So I asked myself, "Could this be a sign from the Lord?" Since we had friends in the circle, it just seemed like everybody knew what was going on between Jamaal and his father except me. A few days later, I got a call from another friend to see how I was doing. She advised me to hold my head up because I did nothing wrong.

Jesus is the best friend you will ever have. I am glad I know Him. He is the one who sent people to encourage me when tears were falling. He held me when I could not sleep. He has been my rock through all this turmoil. At the end of the day,

I can sing, "There is not a friend like the lowly Jesus, no not one."

–Sharon J. Cook

STARTING ALL OVER AGAIN

What do you do when your life begins to change? Take a glance at your life now, where do you go from here? Breathe in the life God chose for you. Life is about choices. You choose a burden because it fits you at that particular moment. But hang on – wait a second, the burden is not yours, it's the Lord's. God said He will cast your concerns into the river of forgetfulness.

There are a number of questions you must ask yourself. Why do we create divisions among ourselves? We know that humanity is recognizing the pain of others. We talk about how to get ahead, instead of how to get closer to God. Why can't we see the world the way God sees it? We need to get it right and keep it tight for the sake of the little people who are watching us. It is important to know that if you don't sacrifice for what you want, your want becomes a sacrifice. One of the most devastating experiences in life is feeling you can't go any further. It is difficult to watch the opportunities in your life fall apart and to lack confidence in your ability to start again. Is there another dream in you to start again? Even if you have made mistakes, you will rise up and get back in the race. Your brokenness is only a bruise that will heal. You are broken to be made stronger. Our struggles are against the evil forces of the world. Strengthen your mind and trust God in the midst of your most miserable times. When you cling to God you will gain strength.

Beginning again is connected to your belief in God. Victory is not an option it's an obligation – God can bless your life.

You have been set up for success, but you must be desperate to succeed and stand firmly on the shoulders of God. When God has a purpose for your life, He will show you how to reach out and get your blessings. Rise above the stumbling blocks. It's your time, the wait is over!

■   ■   ■

Chapter 2

Who Are
You – Really?

What do you know about yourself? This is a question that you should reflect on and take the time to answer. It is essential that we know who we are, what we believe and stand for, our likes and dislikes, our passions, and our fears. Don't be afraid to search your mind and to explore your true self. Doing so will help you make good and positive decisions. Shift some things around, step into a cloud of self-worth. Challenge yourself. Attend some functions, meet people. Push yourself to engage in meaningful conversations.

I made the decision to step out of my comfort zone to write my first book. I stepped into my destiny with God coaching me. Now, I'm writing my second book. My calling has arrived! Taking this step has made me realize that God is allowing me to discover the gifts He has stored in me. Knowing what God has shown me about myself, I can do anything I set my mind to do. My strength and knowledge come from the depth of my soul. I hang out with God and listen to His every word. I am confident that God has big plans for me. My life has a purpose and meaning. I know who I am, and I know where I'm going. I have no doubts about my future.

Do you understand? With God, everything is possible! Take a look at the world today – should we be totally satisfied with the living conditions, job market and economy? There will always be problems. But, are we yearning for better conditions? God is here to show us the way, He will help. However, we have to be willing to do the work. When you lose hope, you stop growing. Teamwork makes dreams come true. God is reality – that's my definition of Him.

We spend a lot of time talking to ourselves and others about changing things. Talk is cheap. Our lives are made up of these three: breakthrough, breakdown and integration. Apply yourself to these three life experiences and watch God meet you at the end of the road.

MAKING IT HAPPEN

Life is a dance between making it happen and letting it happen. You have the power in you to be excellent in every area of your life and the intelligence to do a dance in celebration of your accomplishments. Everything you have has been given to you for a purpose. Use your God-given talents to achieve more and educate others. Don't let your experiences be wasted. Everything you do contains a special purpose. Live your life taking tiny steps. We must redefine success as other than fame and money.

Jesus called us to reconcile, not to condemn each other. Don't judge people. We should be the righteousness of God. Don't feed condemnation. God calls us to minister to people. Have you ever wondered why people don't attend church? Isn't it interesting that Jesus can be a friend of sinners, yet, you say you can't!! Get it in your head today – all of us belong to Jesus.

It's time to get started and live it up for Jesus. You can praise your way to victory. Keep your mind on God. He is amazing!

When you are building an ideal, you need a team of different talents to protect the task you have chosen. Before I retired, I was in charge of the data control department. I needed a team of people who were on the same page that I was on. The goal was to be quick but accurate. In order to carry out the operations, you had to be dedicated to the task at hand. But this would never be discovered until we become disciplined and use the God-given talent we have in us.

Life is the difference between knowing who you are and what you want to happen. You have the power in you to be excellent in every area of your life. Know your talents and express your intelligence in order to do your best. Remember, everything you achieved has a purpose. Use your God given talents to bring comfort to others. Don't let your experiences go to waste.

I know I'm spiritual because the person I've become is nothing compared to the person I was before. God has shown me true love and happiness. I'm at peace with myself because God's love never dies. Look for peace and joy where ever you may be. You will not have to look far. Your soul and heart carry it. Make a point to do something wonderful. Be still and examine yourself. Pay attention to how you talk and walk; work on your imperfections and show your beautiful self. Celebrate the things you can change. Know your destiny, pay attention to your shortcomings. Be quiet sometimes and listen to the whisper of God's message.

FINDING ULTIMATE HAPPINESS

Have you ever turned off the lights in your home, just sat still , cleared your head and let stillness take you into another world? Are you able to see your future? Fill your future with patience and gentleness. Take moments of silence to center yourself. Do you think you have achieved the ultimate happiness you want? Some of us have found that happiness in our homes and that is perfectly fine. If you are to be happy, you must live in the motions of your thoughts and dreams. It's important not to live at the pace of a machine.

In this life, some people have spent a lot of time trying to show others how to attain their happiness. However, in many cases, their true needs are misunderstood. Most of the time, they just want to know that they matter. Use your light to show others the way to God, and He will use you as a vessel – your light will become brighter. We are here to look out for one another as part of a large community. Each of us is here to build, teach, and share. Therefore, the flame we carry should light the way to God's kingdom for the children we are leaving behind.

Yet will I gather others to Him, beside those that are gathered unto him.

(Isaiah 56:8)

In your quest for happiness, don't be self-serving because that takes the spotlight off someone who really deserves to be recognized. Additionally, never be afraid of making mistakes, our most devastating mistakes can serve as a learning tool for our souls. Stay in God's moments, take a back seat and enjoy the ride.

LOVE IN ACTION

Life is not an accident. Do you think your parents will be around forever? If you do – that's not reality. Everyone has to leave this life one day. Sometimes, God has to take you down in order to bring you into a place in your life where you face what is real. Your lifestyle will change, but your destiny should not .So, no matter what happens, keep your destiny upfront and foremost. The key to your happiness is not in someone else's pocket. We can no longer live in history – eternity knows no history.

Eternity is right now. Unfortunately, for many years, we have been carrying pain from generation to generation. But, it's time to put it to rest. It's an energy killer, it serves no purpose. Contrarily, as we get to know God, it is like walking into a light of strength – His energy is shared with us. We are like flowers that when touched by God, open up and prepare for a great tomorrow. The love of God has always been kind and patient.

On March 16, 2015, the owner of Chick-fil-A spoke his mind on traditional marriage and liberals. Gays became unglued. They tried to boycott the restaurant but that was blocked. The restaurant is known for selling foods to hundreds of thousands of supporters. The week the ice storm hit south, cars were stranded for miles. The owner of Chick-fil-A did not close the restaurant. Instead, the restaurant prepared several hundred sandwiches as fast as they could to distribute hot meals to the stranded motorist. Some of the drivers tried to pay him, but he refused to accept the money.

Mr. Pitt explained that his company's policy was based on helping and caring for people. That's why he kept his restaurant open all night into the next day feeding people at no charge.

> For I was hungry and you gave me something to eat: I was thirsty, and you gave me something to drink; I was a stranger and you invited me in.
> (Matthew 25:35)

What Chick-fil-A did was truly generous and heroic – It was a Christian act backed by God's Word.

Some people act out what they are feeling on the inside. When love comes your way, will you act out or shut down? Your journey should be about loving, giving, honesty, respect, and caring.

REGINA'S STORY

Sometimes, we go through life doing what feels good, and simply following others without having a clue of the big picture. According to Regina, there was a time in her life when she was lost, lonely, and unaware of what life was really all about. After being baptized later in life, she thought this was all God expected of her.

"Yes, I went to church but never connected the meaning of life with Christ." She began to realize her life with God was just beginning. "Hearing the Word of God during Sunday morning worship merely pricked my spirit about His will for me." Bits and pieces of information made her question her behavior and the behavior of others. It was only after she acknowledged and realized her sin of adultery that her life changed. She was in love, but with the wrong person and with the wrong intentions. It was as if the Holy Spirit shouted: "You fornicator! What you're doing is wrong." "Feeling quietly ashamed, I soon began to search the Bible for further explanations," she said. Regina read three scriptures from 1 Corinthians:

> Know ye not that the unrighteous shall not inherit the kingdom of God? Be not deceived: neither fornicators, nor idolaters, nor adulterers, nor effeminate, nor abusers of themselves with mankind.
>
> (1 Corinthians 6:9)

Flee fornication. Every sin that a man doeth is without the body.

(1 Corinthians 6:18)

There hath no temptation taken you but such as common to man: but God is faithful, who will not suffer you to be tempted above that ye are able: but will with the temptation always make a way to escape, that ye may be able to bear it. (1 Corinthians 10:13)

These scriptures helped Regina through sad times, and they continue to keep her focused. Her relationship with God was real – talking to Him, asking questions, acknowledging Him, thanking Him, and smiling at the thought of Him. Regina is learning to be patient, obedient, and strong. She has learned to sacrifice her wants and desires and that out of hurt and sadness there is usually joy. "I have learned the joy of loving and learning about the Lord. Hearing from the Lord and reaping the benefits of living His Word are my desires. I can now say that once, I was blind but now, I see. For this and all things, I am truly thankful."

Regina urges everyone to take a few minutes each day to talk to the Lord. He will direct your path and give you peace.

–Regina Bunn

A good friend

LIVE OUTSIDE THE BOX

No matter what happened to us in the past, we are still on a higher plane than before. Friendships and marriages require great commitment and dedication. God put people together for the purpose of serving Him. If God is not in it, get out of it!

God has put me in a place of purification. I have let go of all my insecurities. Now, I wear my pain under the bottom of my shoes – walking in my truth. At the age of ten, I was sexually abused by two family members. That was so horrific and cruel that it put me in a world of disbelief and hatred. As I grew up, my world became more and more tuned into God. I became the person God wanted me to be, and I realized that I am a product of a universe that is fair sometimes and sometimes it's not.

I write to keep myself tuned into the goodness of God. My heart beats to keep me immersed in the very life of human surroundings. Never get too busy making a living that you forget to make a life Because aging is optional but growing old is inevitable. How do you live an ageless life? You can stop announcing your age Otherwise, people will put you in a box or a category. Rather, you should always think of yourself as an individual – healthy, blessed and free to be you. God will not put you in a box. He wants you to expand, move forward, learn good traits, habits, love, and be prosperous. To survive, we must all adapt to change.

■   ■   ■

Chapter 3

As a Man Thinks— So Is He

One day at Frist United Methodist church in Charlotte N.C. a note was left in the offering basket from a homeless person. It read: "Please don't be mad. I don't have much, I'm homeless." That note touched my very soul. Tears just flowed, but you know what? Although he did not have much, he shared what he had. To me, that says a lot about his spirit. How do you feel about your contributions? What's in your heart? In reality, what you think is what you give power to. Thinking the wrong thoughts will put you in an uncomfortable position with God.

Life can be a dream, but it can also be a sailboat. Why do I say that? Because all your dreams can be wiped away in a flash. What do you do when everything disappears? How do you get back on the boat? Trust God, He will take you to a new level. Of course, in this life, there will be challenges; however, you must keep moving forward because everything begins and ends with you. Please don't limit yourself to what you can see with your eyes. You must extend your faith and think positively. God has planted a gift in you to change the world. Try not to compartmentalize your life – that's not God's plan. Grace empowers us to overcome whatever we are going through, so fill your life with grace. Let God use you supernaturally. Don't think for one moment that God cannot use you because others may not like you, God loves people, and uses those who are not liked and have been discarded by others. Those are the ones He pays keen interest in. God will build them a mountain of blessings, and He will make sure they persevere in the most awesome way.

Don't get involved with people who label you because they don't know what God has in store for you. Behind every gift, there is a price to pay, and you must always be mindful not to get caught up in who people say you are. Rather, you need to focus on who God says you are – prayer changes things. I can testify of that because He has brought me a mighty long way, and I still have a long way to go – He is not finished with me yet.

JEANETTE'S STORY

Growing up I had a serious attitude problem. It was my way or no way. I could care less about anybody's feelings but my own. One day, I was approached by someone who asked me, what I wanted out of life. Being the type of person I was with an indifferent attitude and a smart mouth, I replied: "Why does that concern you? That's none of your business." His reply was, "With that attitude you will not get very far." I shrugged it off. As time went on, it seemed like everything in my life was going wrong. I began to think about the con-versation I had and I started to pray and ask God why me? Not knowing it was all me. I prayed and ask God to help me change my life and attitude.

One day, someone else approached me with the same ques-tion. I was truly amazed. It shocked me, but what came out of my mouth was all positive – no smart mouth, no attitude. But I was very sincere. I said, I wanted to be a better person, respectful and helpful to others where possible. I have learned from many mistakes. Most of all, I've given God the praise. Truly, God stepped in and gave me a giant attitude adjustment.

God has definitely gotten me out of some bad situations and by His grace, I am here to talk about it. Prayer changes all things – just trust, believe, and you too will prevail.

—Jeanette Carter-Merritt

Allow God to use His supernatural power.

RISING ABOVE YOUR PROBLEMS

What do you do when you pray for something, and God says "NO"? You pray for everybody, give good advice, and you praise God with all your heart, yet, God still says "NO." It's very simple, it's not your time. Whatever you think you deserve, God has the last word. You have been overruled. Continue to live righteously. Be the person God says you are. God said His grace is sufficient to handle anything. He will not command us to do something without giving us the means to do it. Take what God puts in you out into the world. God wants us to put a smile on His face. He will trust you with troubles because you have passed the test of time.

Truth is, you are no saint, all the assumptions you have made in your life are about how you feel. However, we have so much going on in our lives, we don't know if we are doing the best we can.

The devil is everywhere – lurking, plotting, and looking for the next opportunity to make someone's life miserable. Don't get me wrong: the devil appears to be giving you great blessings, but in the end, what he gives are always filled with traps. The Devil is in churches where you are least likely to find him.

I was a witness of a problem, one morning a lady came to church late as usual and wanted a lady to move further down the pew, so she could sit at the end. The lady stepped into the aisle to let her in. She instantly had an attitude. You could see she was upset. Be mindful that the lady came in after the service had started. The devil is always busy. Why can't people act accordingly and be an example for others? You are always being watched, check your attitude and make the adjustments. Set boundaries. Remember life is ten percent what happens to you, and ninety percent what you do about it.

When you are going through crisis, remove yourself from the situation, go for a walk, do something fun. Then come back and adjust yourself, so you will be in the moment of what's happening in your life. If people allow themselves to face their fears of the unknown, their future will be much happier and promising. When things fall apart, take the high road, rise above your problems, take the calling God has put on your life. People have the idea that God will swoop in and take care of all their problems but that's not going to happen. God wants you to invest in Him, He wants your trust and love. Make no mistake, your problems are never your own, there are always people involved in your life who have something to do with the decisions you make.

SELF-IMPROVEMENT

Let's talk about self-improvement. What do you think makes you fully aware of who you are? Do you think self-awareness is the key to finding oneself? Learn to embrace your authentic self. You are who you are because of where you came from. If you want to re-discover yourself, look further than your inner being. Shake up the family tree. Dig deep into your family history. Tap into the souls of your older relatives. Ask the hard questions: Who am I? What makes me curious? Where did I get my personality? And who do I look like? Get to know your history. Move on to bigger and better desires.

Sometimes, we refuse to give change a chance. Are we afraid of the changes that are already here? (Stay with me). We no longer live in the season where change is welcome. We must learn to accept what we don't understand. Change is not to break us; change is here to make us better. Change is a part of life. Something always happens when God gets a hold of us. We begin to think for ourselves. We become hungry for education; we even begin standing on our own. This is the power of God working on our behalf.

I was invited to Waters A.M.E church with Pastor Charles Baugh, his lovely wife Diane Baugh and the women's circle. The atmosphere at Waters church was overwhelming – so spiritual and welcoming. We discussed the book I wrote, *My Journey to Freedom*. What an amazing group of fine, outstanding women. The room was filled with the presence of God. The conversation was filled with truth and joy and there were questions. The women were eager to speak on subjects mentioned in the book. Knowing that someone had experienced the same ordeals, gives others reasons to go on and be better persons. I could feel the energy in the room. To actually sit and speak with someone who has been through so many negative things yet comes out with a positive outlook on life was amazing. That was one the most wonderful reading and speaking sessions I have encountered. I give my heart to the women of Waters A.M.E church. Stay blessed.

My greatest wish is to stay positive and truthful to my God. It's a great joy to spread the Word of my Lord and Savior. God can only come in your life if you invite Him. Don't be afraid to push harder toward your greatness. God does not look at your outer body. He looks into your heart and soul. Our lives and services belong to God. Once you get a mere glance of God and feel His presence, you will feel the grace of God filling your very soul. God is every breath we take. Be submissive to God, we must reconnect ourselves to Him. To be present in this world at this particular time, is a wonder. Life is wonderful don't cheat yourself.

The beauty of learning is loving your passion. Take a moment, and think about what will lift your spirit. When we long for goodness and guidance, we focus on our leaders. We go to church to hear the Word spoken by our spiritual leaders. We believe our spiritual leaders are chosen by God to lead us to Him.

Isn't it strange that most of us go home put our Bibles and thoughts of God on a shelf until the next Sunday? WRONG! WRONG! WRONG! on every level. Do you realize God is watching you? What if God treated you that way? Where would you be? Think about this. Read your Bible, stay in tune with the Word of God.

Do you believe Satan and the ego are one in the same? We refuse to see the evil in ourselves. Grace is very powerful. If you follow grace, it will help you understand your way of thinking. You are more than a thought. Grace teaches you how special you are. Follow grace with peace, joy, and contentment. Seek peace when someone has wronged you. Forgive quickly, God will handle your situation.

God makes the rain fall on the just and the unjust. You can't place yourself on a higher level than your fellow man. Don't give anyone your power by retaliating. Take a breather, step back and assess. Create a loving response in order to keep your power.

As I greet others, I pray silently for each person. I pray for peace. I pray to God to use me in every way possible. When God allows people to come into my life, it's only for a reason and a season. Please don't try to hold on to something or someone whom God is moving in a different direction. If you are carrying a backpack of grudges and hatred, your back will become more and more bent over with frustration.

Life is so short and precious not to enjoy it. I have learned to embrace my imperfections because aging causes a decrease in my values, I look at myself as an ageless goddess. I'm loyal to God, a trend setter, I build boundaries, and create good habits. It does not matter to me what people say because I'm working on getting to heaven. I know I'm on the right track – or I'm just plain delusional.

We all have a purpose; we are here as symbols. Do you know you are not your thoughts? There are amazing things that surround you. Your experience with life is something wonderful. What would we find if we look beyond our thoughts? Will it be a better version of ourselves? God gave us thoughts, peace, joy, integrity, and the will to explore and learn. What have you gotten from God's teachings? The energy God gave us, we must use it to move in His direction. We are here for a deep purpose, to love, live, and multiply.

COMING OF AGE SPIRITUALLY

It is a joy to come of age spiritually. It's amazing, every waking moment is a new beginning, every handshake is a new hello. Because each day, a page of your life is deleted. Live life with full joy. Live your life with high energy. Rule out hypercritical and strengthen your relationship with God.

I sincerely think most of us are afraid of how we will die as opposed to when we will die. The focus of my prayer is asking God to give me the strength to live the life He prepared for me. We are here to serve.

There are many people who are suffering from loneliness or despair, or living in the past. See the truth as it is, look the Devil in the eye, put him in his place. You should know you control your thoughts. Meditation is a way of keeping yourself on the right track. Let God be your driver. Don't keep punishing yourself. It's not a man's world, it's your life, get a grip. What happened in the past cannot be changed. The only thing you can do is change the way you live in the future.

Learn the four agreements:

1. Be impeccable with your word
2. Don't take anything personally
3. Don't make assumptions
4. Always do your best

The greatest gift you can give is forgiveness. It will set you free to go on to greater endeavors. Take the responsibility for bringing good energy to the people who you love and care for.

I wrote my first book because it served as healing for me. I wrote my own truth. When you recognize what mistakes you have made in your life, it's like a lightbulb going off. You finally understand the reason you went through all the ups and downs. Now, it's time to take control. Let God lead you to the promise land.

We all know that we were saved by grace and delivered from judgment. When God was on the cross, He said: "It is done." That means God has covered all our sins. When you speak the Word of God, your faith releases itself into where ever it needs to go. Jesus lives on the inside of us. Make the Devil tremble. Give your heart and soul to Jesus.

To see God in someone who is doing you wrong is the true power in you. Coming from God, trust me this task is extremely hard. But, we as servants of God must learn to make alternative decisions. God will show you how to deliver yourself out of this hold and bring you into a clear meaning of life.

MAKING EVERY MOMENT COUNT

Let's turn the human race into a human family. Be a spirited leader, let grace awaken you to the holy power, which comes from the highest power ever imagined. When you find the grace of peace, you will be able to face anything. This life is not about you; it's about serving God's purpose. God has ordained each of us to do great things. I may not be able to do all He has ordained me to do in this body but as I approach the end of my life, I know my next transition will be with God. My purpose is to take this journey with the greatest amount of joy.

People can talk you out of some things, but they can't talk you out of your experiences. I gave myself to God so He can use me. Isn't it mind blowing how God shows up when you least expect Him?

Why not talk about why you are here? When you are sailing in the same direction of your purpose – stay in harmony. You have remarkable powers, use them to grow in the direction God has mapped out for you. Don't allow the powers to lay dormant. Excite the very essence of the soul! Never stop learning about yourself but always tap into the very breath of every waking moment.

Your authentic powers will tell you how wonderful and creative you are, but remember, there will come a time when your beauty will not turn heads. When your looks fade and you lose confidence, just look back to see how far you've come. Take the high road and grow old gracefully. It's not the end of the world. Every choice you make will have consequences. Make decisions and lay foundations wisely.

If you have a genuine partner, they should be able to help you face all that you are longing for, you may need a little push in the right direction or a word of encouragement. Sometimes, we need to approach life with the word, just stand still and watch God perform. The love and healing of God are there. Reach for them, embrace them, and cherish them. It's time.

■   ■   ■

Chapter 4

Finding Your Higher Self

The love of God will truly amaze you. Have you ever thought about how great the loneliness would be without God? How would you embrace failures and pitfalls? That is certainly something to think about. Living a spiritual life – does that give you harmony and peace? Ask yourself those questions.

If you have taken the time and money to educate yourself, then the answers to your questions should be no-brainers. If where you are now is any indication of how far you have come – whether it's being highly educated or having a high school diploma – it does not matter as long as you consider yourself successful in your own right.

Learn how to survive change. God will love you above and beyond your mistakes. God uses us when we don't have a clue what's going on. When you give your soul to God, in return, He gives you serenity. That's the joy and pleasure you get for being the person God has carved out for you. God's light is like a ray of sunshine coming from the depths your soul. It enhances you to become a person of humility, someone who is responsible with love and respect. This is a gift that comes from the soul of our maker.

How do you find your higher self? I know you will have to go deep within your soul to find that person. Are you obedient to self? What connects you to the higher power? When you begin to arm yourself with the higher power; you challenge pain, hurt, sadness, and other opposition. If you say yes to God, the healing is on its way. By now, you should be armed and ready to go out on the limb for God. Just think about all the burdens God has allowed you to bear – all the devils came at you. Who do you think blocked those unhealthy anxieties? Get real people. God is the only way.

I firmly believe, we are all instinctively connected. God created ways for us to live to please Him. In return, we get the pleasures of living more fruitful and peaceful lives. Our journey is to eliminate fear, but without God, it's totally impossible. Our roads must be orchestrated by God and God alone.

MY ENCOUNTER WITH GOD

I had an encounter with God. This particular time in my life was filled with burdens, turmoil and rejection. Before I went to bed that night, I asked God to come see about me. I will never forget what He did. His eyes were such an incredible blue; there's no color blue in this world that comes close. His eyes were as round as a saucer. When I woke up, I was as light as a feather. All my fears, worries, despair, and anxieties had disappeared. I praised God all day. I never looked back. My belief in God has never been shaken.

You only have authority in your own space. I have learned from all my mistakes and have not hidden from them. I will not unload my burdens or my mistakes on others. When you feel good about owning your own mistakes, it is such a great relief – knowing you have obeyed God's will. Authenticity is a great source of giving, loving, and kindness – be grateful for all your missteps.

NEVER ALONE

Praise God when you are feeling good or bad. Keep pressing on toward the mark God has prepared for you. God will slow down your progress just to make sure you don't arrive or receive your blessings too soon. Receiving a blessing too soon can be devastating for you. Take the stairs and not the elevator, stay the course and take it slowly.

God has the power to bring you out. Who is your closest companion? God will be in you, upon you, and with you all the days of your life. This is the kind of comfort you want in your life; He will fill you in every area of your life.

> But the fruit of the Spirit is love, joy, peace, longsuffering, gentleness, goodness, faith, meekness, temperance: against such there is no law.
>
> (Galatians 5:22-23)

This passage tells you what He will produce in you. If you live the life God has for you, He will become your companion, bridge over troubled waters, your provider and everything you need. When you begin to operate out of the Holy Spirit, you will be surprised. God will never let you walk alone. He knows where you are and what you are thinking. He has guided you all of your life, ordering your steps, knocking down walls, laying down solid grounds, and positioning you to be blessed.

Think about how God has guided your future. He wiped tears away, helped you raise your children, provided you with a job, put your children through school and college and nurtured you. Wake up people! God is in charge. You are guided by the Almighty Light.

You are here because God planned for you to be here. Your steps have been ordered. Put away evil, and self- doubt because you are in the hands of my God. Learn to let God take control – allow Him to move you to the next level.

FOCUS ON GOD'S AGENDA

God will not give you a dream if He thought you could not fulfill it. You should set your goals for beyond tomorrow. You should never cement yourself in any situation. Keep stirring up the juices in your life.

God creates deliverers for the purpose of helping others to make a comeback. We all want to be heard and valued. God uses shaky people to make sturdy people. Find your passion for your life. If that thing haunts you long enough that your passion wants to be exposed give in to it, exercise it, and bring it to real life. That's God pushing you into your goals. Only you know the path to your own truth. Where you are now – that's the road map God circled for you. We all yearn to be seen and heard.

Why do people concern themselves with what people think of them? We should look at ourselves and go with our talents and ambitions. God gave each of us a mind. Pay attention to the agenda He prepared for you. We all have choices. Find the happiness and the place that makes you joyful and fulfilled. Strive toward your potential. You cannot have a harvest if you don't sow a seed. Fight for your goals.

Are you living with a yoke around your neck? It may be bitterness toward someone, lack of confidence, or a bad relationship. It could be anything that burdens you down. If you are not careful you could pass it down from generation to generation. Nevertheless, you can destroy the yoke and agree with God that the buck stops here. Listen to the Word of God; give your burdens to Him and He will remove all your yokes and burdens – He will set you free! You are important to Him – He made you, not to struggle but to prosper. You have now made a decision to honor Him. That's your ticket to happiness. Accelerate, don't procrastinate. Put your faith in action.

LIVE THE LIFE GOD INTENDED

In the world today, we cannot assume we are the rulers. Think of all the billions of people who made this country what it is now. You are the master of your fate and the captain of your soul. If we go through life being selfish and self- centered, what chance will our children have? We must show love toward our fellow man. We can build a world of joy, peace, and harmony. We know what God has instilled in us. We were not put here to judge or create commotion. We must live the ultimate life God intended for each of us.

Getting started on trying to attain the crown God has waiting for us is not easy. We must govern ourselves as people of God. To do this, we must show our gratitude toward everything God has blessed us with, work for God and not for ourselves or others. Give your mind, heart, and soul to Him. Recognize you are not here by chance, but God ordered you to be here.

Don't give up a chance to see our Lord and Savior some-day. Live in a way to make Him want to come back for you. Trust me, you don't want to live outside of the spirit, you want to live inside of the spirit. Let God tame your heart.

Be a blessing to someone. It's not hard, work on your inner self and then work on your outer self. It takes time, I did it and so can you. Talk to God regularly, He has a lot to say, so just listen and be His servant. He can make your life a living paradise. Take it from me, I've been to the mountain top and down to the valley. It's no fun falling from on high. I'm trying to save somebody from the wrath God holds in His hands. Everybody's situation is different, but everybody comes with burdens.

HOLD ON TO GOD'S HANDS

My story is like everyone else's. I look back and see all the obstacles, hurt, pain, and anguish I put myself through. Not knowing all I had to do was STOP, LOOK, AND LISTEN. The thought of it makes me want to hit myself upside the head. All of that could have been avoided. Look at your life, make godly changes. God is a God of many chances, don't delay do it now while you still have a chance.

If I had changed my life long ago, I can only imagine that the accomplishments, the joy and peace I have now, I could have had then. I will not give it up for all the money in the world. God has told me, if I follow His Word and put Him first, He will give me joy, prosperity, love, and happiness. God did not have to save me, but He saw something in me worth nurturing. He worked with me and watched me grow into a person with great belief – I gave my life to God, and I never looked back.

Here is the clinger – you will lose relationships. But that's OK, I can live with that. I cannot serve man and God. I've gained so much more than I lost. How many of you know what I'm talking about? Don't let anyone hold you back from being one of God's anointed ones. Take hold of God's hand and let Him make your life a grand production. Every time I want to do something spectacular, I step out in faith.

In the midst of praying, God is always lifting and pushing me into my destiny. I can feel His presence and I can almost touch His very hand. I wrapped myself in His goodness. I am faithful to God. He has always shown me mercy and favor. Try Him; He is an awesome God.

■   ■   ■

Chapter 5

Never, Ever Give Up

If you are in a difficult situation, and it seems like there is no way out – don't give up! Move steadfastly forward – never looking back. God put you on that track, there will not be any roadblocks. Being obedient is the key to unlocking the doors. Oh, by the way, reach back and give a helping hand. It's what God expects from you.

My friend Arthur and I attend the Kappa Alpha affair, which he has been a member of for fifty years. I have seen men in the organization with such politeness and respect. They wear their uniforms with such dignity and honor, it is amazing. For the most part, the affairs are well put together and very well attended. Sometimes, I wonder if the younger generation will continue to carry the torch the seniors have lit for them. When I look at other organizations that have fallen, I tremble with sadness trying to understand the reason for their failure.

I ask myself, "Who let the Devil in?" We all realize he is standing by waiting to destroy. When God is in the building, no devil in hell can upset or re-organize anything God put together. It may bend, but it will not break. These organizations build character and integrity in young men and women; they set them on a road to greatness, to achieve out-standing goals.

When we are tossed and driven on the restless sea of time; we often wonder which road to take. God will guide us to the place of greatness. Young men, young women, take God by the hand, He will stabilize you, lead you, and comfort you. Success is waiting for you.

WHEN GOD SEEMS FAR AWAY

In 1958, we held a Thursday night dance at Harvey Johnson High school, which was on the opposite side of the bridge. I was not allowed to attend unless my brothers were with me. During that time, there were different names for sections of south Baltimore: Lee Street Bridge and Handover Street Bridge and Sharp Street. I lived on the opposite side of both. During school, my brother James and another guy had an exchange of words. The next school day, James and the guy got into an altercation, which led to another exchange of words, and it soon became a battle. The fight escalated out of school to Fremont Ave and Pace Street, which was on the opposite side of the bridge – with so many boys involved, it seemed like a war zone. There were sticks, bottles, and cans. It seemed as if a hundred boys were throwing punches. That was the biggest fight I have ever witnessed. The police were not called, nobody was sent to the hospital, no guns or knives were involved. I don't remember if there was a truce called. In school the next day no one spoke of it. That was a little strange to me. Today, it would have been very different. In those days, no one carried long-term anguish.

What do you do when it seems faith has failed you? What do you do when you are a good parent, and try to raise your child to stay out of trouble and things still go wrong? People will look at you saying, "Where is your God now?" We live between two voices, one is telling you your faith has failed you, the other is telling you about desertion. Have you been put on trial? Sometimes, in your life, you will ask, where is God? It's a shame to go to church every Sunday and not have faith. You ask God, "Where were you in my disappointments?" But God is sitting on the throne preparing to heal you of all your pain. Nobody in this world can say they have never been through upsetting painful situations. But in those times you must wait on the Lord for He is coming back. This is the will of God.

God is the Author and the Finisher of our faith. Have you ever done something that did not reflect who you are? God put something in you that the world is going to need. God is the source of everything. He loves for you to trust Him and rely on Him. God doesn't need your help; He needs your trust. God wants you to make Him your priority.

Have you thought about your happiness? Own it, you wrote the script – you can change the journey. See yourself as the most valuable, loyal, irresistible person God has ever put together. Enjoy your relationship with yourself. If God decided to put someone in your life, they can join the party. Can you balance work and play? We all have battles. God has taught us how to overcome our problems. Give your problems to God. What's most important is not what you leave for people, it's what you leave in them.

We all have battles but have you ever wondered why bad things happen to good people? The truth is, your righteousness will still bring you pain. You may ask yourself, where did

I go wrong? Why am I being short changed? These are the questions that challenge your faith. What do you do when you have fallen? Somewhere in your life, your faith has been put on trial. You have the Devil on one shoulder and an angel on the other and now, you are in limbo wondering which way is up. Who do you listen to? Be careful about your decision. One wrong move will place you in a position you cannot fight your way out of. Devils can be cunning and fearful – you cannot sleep with the enemy and call yourself free.

Have you ever called for God and He did not answer? Just like a great bottle of wine, He makes you sit to make you better. God preserves you to get the best out of you.

MY COUSIN'S STORY

My cousin revealed to me some horrible things that happened to her. Mary and her sister were walking through a dark alley when they saw a person with a cigarette. They turned around and ran. She was struck by a car, and it caused her to roll over onto the pavement. She got up with only a scratch. She knew God was there. From that time on, she prayed that God would help them get a better apartment in a safer area.

Between the age of 16 and 18, her prayer was answered and she lived in a better house than before. She grew up around drugs, alcohol, gambling, and prostitution. She continued to pray for a better life. At the age of 16, she got pregnant and dropped out of school. Struggling to take care of a baby was not easy for her. Later on, she went back to high school and did obtain her twelfth-grade diploma. She completed computer training and landed a good job. She kept praising God every step of the way.

She met a wonderful man and got married at the age of thirty – one of the best things that could have happened to her. God opened her eyes to see that the people whom she thought would be happy for her, became jealous, envious, and deceitful. God was still working on her.

At the age of fifty-seven, her husband became very ill and was on life support for ten months. She prayed for God to keep her strong. God never failed, He kept His promise.

She received a letter from IRS – it was a huge tax bill. She put it in her Bible and prayed to God to help her. A month later, the bill was cut in half and the payments were very low. Two months later, her husband was off life support and he came home. While taking care of her husband; she became depressed and could not sleep at night. She made an appointment to see her doctor; he prescribed sleeping pills. The next morning, not paying close attention, she took a sleeping pill instead of her blood pressure medication. She fell asleep at the wheel on a busy street. She went over the median strip into traffic going in the opposite direction and landed in some bushes in someone's front yard.

The police officer and paramedics rushed her to the hospital. The doctor examined her and ran tests including a cat scan and she had no physical injuries. Her truck on the other hand was totally wrecked. Again, God was working it out. Mary's husband passed away five years later after thirty-one years of marriage. Mary states, "I'm still here and being blessed by the mighty hands of God."

Mary Newman is my beautiful cousin whom I love very deeply. What a brave and courageous God-fearing woman.

REMEMBER THE CHILDREN

Take a look at your situation but don't stare at it too long because the more you worry the less you will believe God is in the midst. Sometimes, we just think too much about things that belong to God. Let's face it, you cannot do anything about your turmoil until you turn it over to God. Do yourself a favor and talk to God. After all, we are all trying to get to the promised land. Everybody talks about going to heaven, unfortunately, some of us will not get there. People who have faith grow old more gracefully. It may not stop injuries, but it hastens the process.

Put on the helmet of hope, faith, and prosperity. Stay in control of your joy. Where your mind goes you will follow. Be determined to keep your mind on Jesus. Think about all the good God has done for you. Stay in the circle of the Father, Son, and the Holy Ghost.

The thing about purpose is, what goes around will come around – this is just to remind you of how you treated others when you had the power in your hand. Be careful not to destroy feelings. Life has its valleys. You may become vulnerable and have to rely on the very person you were horrible to. Be big enough to see the bigger purpose for your life and have the will to recover.

Our children are sending us messages. Young people want a chance, and they feel no one cares, is listening or feel their pain. Our young people have talents, they want us to recognize and nurture them. We should see the greatness in our children, they need our guidance. Our future depends on them. As parents, teachers, and political leaders, we must recognize the pain our children are carrying. They could be anyone's child, just take the initiative and lend a helping hand to guide them in a positive direction.

Stop lying to those children, be transparent. You know you have not been saved all your life – Let those children know you are not a saint. Your life was saved after you stopped lying, cheating, ducking, hiding, backsliding, smoking, and coking, chasing and in every hole and corner, from pillow to post, trying to be something you were not. They don't need to know all that. Children just need to know that making a mistake is not the end of the world. Mistakes will be forgiven, don't punish them for what they don't know – only for what they deliver. Explain to your children the principles of God. Show them what happens when you are obedient to God. Live a godly life in front of them. God will guide you the rest of the way.

BEWARE OF PRIDE AND THE DEVIL

Don't feed into pity and hopelessness; give up pity parties. You can be pitiful or powerful, but you can't have both. Get real, life is not lonely even if you are the only one believing in God; He has a plan for you. We are the hope in a dark world. Hold on to your anchor because the Devil is always lurking – give him a run for his money. We are the anchors of our souls. We should expect something good to happen each day. Don't sell yourself short, stop giving your life to others. Self-reliance should be where God wants it, not in the hands of others. Take a big stand, you are God's most precious creatures, love and protect yourself from Satan. He comes in nice suits and beautiful dresses, always in the finest. Recognize who is in your group and around you. Stop, look and listen.

God will not cut you off if you don't bear fruit. He will hold you up until you are able to stand on your own. Never think because you don't have something to give, you are not worthy to go into God's house. The devil is a liar. Stay true to God. He will grant you the true meaning of giving and serving Him. You matter to God.

Do you realize when you strut, you stumble? Please don't take anything for granted. If you find yourself beating your chest for something you thought you did that's when God steps in and catches you off guard. If there is anything great happening in your life, please give God the glory and praise. You will be much happier when you recognize that God is the reason.

Sometimes, so many of us wonder why it takes so long to get where we want to be. God moves the faithful into the lives of the unfaithful. Remember, God uses His people to bring the unfaithful to Him. Don't ever think you are not being used one way or another by God. Those people who wear crosses around their necks that are big enough to kill the break of daylight and carry Bibles – who are they trying to impress? God knows their hearts and what they are up to before they do. So what's the point? If it's not to glorify God then stop wasting your time. All you are doing is playing into Satan's hands.

You are better than that. Know your place, correct your life, lift yourself up and respect the Word of God. Take my advice – avoid the foolishness. At some time in your life, take a positive stand. Don't settle for just enough, grow in truth. If you think sitting in church every Sunday sub-noising people, talking bad about others and thinking you are better is fine, you are mistaken. That is not at all appealing to God. I see weak areas in some churches, don't get me wrong no one is perfect. Nevertheless, God reminds us what sin is. We sometimes commit sin in our lives. If you don't know how to address people without making them feel small, then you need serious prayer. Get off your high horse and put yourself in the other person's shoes. Never think you are in a better place or better off than the next person. God will always have a plan for you. The lack of respect for others will never be ok with God.

PAIN, SHAME, AND LIES

Some people will take advantage of your uncertainties. When your pain is created by others, it cuts deep, God has exactly what you need, it's called the language of pray. You have to worship your pain away. When you learn to worship and give God your worries and when it's all said and done, your pain will fade like the dew on a sunshiny day.

Shame is something we dwell on. It will cause self-doubt, it will bring your spirits down and leave you empty. God has a remedy for your shame. He will take away your scars and the unfair things you endure. Put your shoulders back, hold your head up, and don't struggle with your problems. Value yourself, don't let anybody devalue you. You are not a mistake in God's eyes. This is your day of freedom. God will pay you back for the injustice you suffered. Keep on praying, God will bring you out better than you were before. Hold to God's everlasting words; He will calm every storm in your life.

I found out the devil will lie to you if you choose to listen. I know why I serve God. God has a purpose for my life. When I learned how God wanted me to serve Him, there was no turning back. The fight was on. I took a long look at myself and said: "It's you and me Lord, all the way." I stepped into my creativeness, took the world by the tail and became the person God wanted me to be. When you make a decision to let God lead you, no Devil in hell can stop you from your destiny. The will of God becomes so powerful, you can't think about turning back.

WAIT ON THE LORD

God caught me at a very devastating time of my life. It was like a piece of flying debris that caught me in a very dangerous zone. I'm sharing this with people who I feel earned the right to hear my story.

My peace was nestled under a pile of hate, loneliness, sadness, regret, and confusion. I did not know how to retrieve happiness. The grace of God stepped in and saved me at a moment that could have destroyed my very spirit. It was like a dam bursting open, washing all the dirt, hurt, shame, and regrets away. When you believe in the power of faith, and not the power of fear, there is nothing you can't conquer. You are half way home. God has taught me to recognize prosperity and grace.

Low moments will show you who you are. Have you ever found yourself balled up in a corner crying? Not knowing what to do or where to go? You ask yourself: "Is there a lesson God wants me to learn from this?" But, you trust God. What I said to God is: "I trust you, I am hurting. I know there is a better life in store for me. I know my heart is protected by you. I'm sheltered by the Shepherd." I was trapped by pain hoping God would bring me out. I took the high road and leaned on Him. God was waiting for me to say the word. I asked Him to deliver me and cover me with His mercy. God covered me like a mother bird covers her eggs. God brought me out of many burning buildings.

What do you do when your soul cries out, "Lord, I am weary of the loads I'm carrying. The business of living has drained the life out of me. I don't think I can face another day. My body needs rest; my mind needs rest; even my spirit needs rest. I need to be renewed from the inside out." And He says, "Wait." Wait upon the Lord, and He shall renew your strength. "Oh, God bring the river of your life to me. Let it flow and refresh every weary worn out place in me. Thank you Lord for your grace and mercy."

■　■　■

Chapter 6

Overcoming the Battles of Life

My sisters and brothers most of us come to the Lord damaged and dead spiritually, damaged emotionally, and decaying physically. When He saved you, He made your dead spirit come alive. He began the massive renovation necessary to repair your damage thoughts about life, about others, and about yourself. Beneath our pasted-on smiles and pleasant greetings, we alone hear the rumblings of the midnight shift. God is constantly excommunicating lethal thoughts that hinder us from grasping the many-faceted callings and giftings buried beneath the rubble of our minds. We all need the Lord to help us with ourselves.

When God speaks to you in your spirit. Don't run to get your Bible to read a scripture. Because God is the author. Listen to me people – God wants you to read His Word in order to keep the communication lines open. God will send His angels to accommodate all your needs. Allow Him to defeat all forces that come your way. God will always be your protector. God will detour you from accidents, and fatal destruction, you just need to trust Him.

We all try to have that godly experience in a worldly world. Some people get themselves together at an early age. Getting rid of childish things does not heal everybody the same way or at the same time. Sometimes, we become judge and jury over afflicted people. You could be operating under false pretense. God will send someone to bring you to Jesus. We don't know who they are. God uses the words "they" and "them" all through the Bible. They should not be important to us as long as we obey and cooperate with God's Word. God has performed many miracles in our lives. Yet, some of us continue to be disobedient to His Word. We wake up every day knowing what God has faithfully done in our lives, and yet, we still don't trust Him. Are we so blind we can't see God's blessings?

EXPECT A BREAKTHROUGH

When trouble and desperation fall upon us, we turn to the Lord without hesitation. Are you willing to challenge your perception? Our lives are like a movie with lots of scenes. Things may go well for a while then all hell breaks loose. But wait – you have many tasks to perform. Hold on to your dreams. No one can change God's plans for your life. We may not be able to understand all God is doing, but just be calm, don't get discouraged. Don't let your upsets take your mind off your goals. Things will shift in your favor. God wants to stabilize you and move you to a greater power of peace. You will come to a victorious finish.

Jesus knew His final scene was not being on the cross. He knew his final scene would be determined by God. God is the supply house for everybody. Your life is worthy of the pleasantries of life. God is good to us, because He is good and perfect, no man should come before Him.

When you learn how to rest that's when God does His best. Have you been caught in a battle, that's not about you? Some people will take their troubles and lay them on you. You have no idea why they are lashing out at you. You are living in the criticism of someone else's problems. Anytime you don't fit in the institution of criticism, they would consider throwing you out of their group. You have to understand the enemy in order to live in this world. You have to know where to put them in your life. Either you discredit them or put them out of your life. Everybody is not going to celebrate you. Do what you know is right. All criticism is not bad. Some criticisms are given to help lift you up, when you acknowledge your critics, you strategize carefully. Be careful when choosing your friends, some people are not who they say they are.

When the storm is raging, only God can calm it. If passive faith touches hands with aggressive faith, it creates a vision of angels ready to come to conquer your crises. When grace gets you out of a situation, please make haste, stop lying around in anger. If you see the light, walk toward it, get out of your situation, make a brand new start. Don't let anything stand between you and your breakthrough. The gate is open.

GOD'S MIGHTY HAND

Before you realize it, sometimes God has already done the amazing thing He promised. Remember when Pharaoh's men were after the Israelites? The Israelites had nowhere to go. Yet, Moses told the people to go forward. But how could they go forward when the Red Sea stood between them and the other side? Out of nowhere, a strong wind parted the sea. Just when you think you have nowhere to go, God will make a way right on time. God will stand by your side in good times and bad.

You have experienced the difference between God and Satan. God gives you love; Satan gives you misery. God is sovereign! What will it take to give your life to Him? We cannot see into the future. Our trust in God should not be limited. He has the ability to change our lives in a split second. He can eliminate bad things that are headed our way. Left up to us, we can never stop the trouble that's coming our way. One day we will all have to face God. People, listen to God, fear Him, and turn away from wrong doings. Living for God is the only way you will have a sense of peace. Trust Him and live the life of abundance. Make the change now and bring someone with you. Things will only get better if you walk with God. He will not turn you away.

Do you want to take a journey to wholeness? Do you hunger for God's touch? "God, I am hungry for your touch. I will follow your footsteps. If I'm blind, I can follow your voice. Allow me to bend my knees, so I can bow down and praise your holy name. God, I accept you in my heart. Jesus come and live inside me. God, predestine me to become more like your son Jesus. Take my soul and mold me, make me the person you want me to be. Guide me, purify me, lift me up. Show me how to be more deserving of your love." Out of my brokenness has proceeded wholeness.

I have worked hard to fill my life with gratitude, patience, love, respect, and generosity. We are not here for a long time, we are here to have a good time worshiping God and following His commands.

I was invited to a graduation party, before I entered the building I prayed that everyone would be loving and grateful to God for being able to celebrate the young lady's achievements. It was such a calming experience to know God was in the building. I felt His presence. A little prayer has a powerful effect. The young lady was excited and pleasantly surprised.

THE POWER OF FORGIVENESS

God loves us enough not to leave us in bad situations. Don't be angry at the people who treated you unfairly. Step aside and let God take hold of the situation. Let God know you are available to do His will. God has a perfect plan for your life. Stay in tune with His presence and rest in His love. God is getting ready to turn some things around in your life. He can touch a billion souls at once, and never overlook one person. God is the key to unlocking all the precious gifts He has for your life.

Give us this day our daily bread. Be bold enough to ask God to forgive you. God forgives us our debts as we forgive those who have debts against us. You have to show God your works by faith. You should not do what is right only to be saved, you should do what is right because you are saved. The more privileges you have, the more responsibilities you have. Look to God for help. He will not put more on you than you can handle. God has pulled you out of so many dangerous situations, it should be easy to trust Him and forgive others.

God loves us enough not to leave us in bad situations. Don't get angry at the people who treated you unfairly. Take a step aside and let God take hold of the situation. Let God know you are available to do His will. God has a perfect plan for your life. Stay in His presence, rest in His love. God is getting ready to turn some things around in your life. God can touch a billion souls at once, never overlook one person. God is the key to unlocking all the precious gifts in your life.

Has someone every insulted you without a reason? Surely, you can find it in your heart to forgive them. Here is the thing – if you cannot forgive the bad side, you won't get to see the positive side. Don't bind yourself down with revenge and hatred. Spend your time looking for leverage. Be the bigger person, don't spend your time wallowing in dislike and discontentment, release the anger – you are poisoning your very soul. Celebrate the new found grounds of your faith. James 2 states, "Do not hold the faith of our Lord Jesus Christ, the Lord of glory with partiality." Choosing the right attitude can make all the difference in your walk with God. Once you have made a commitment to God, it is natural to want to reach out to others like yourself. Accepting the rejected is not a weakness of the people; it is a strength. Neither can we shelter hardened criminals who are content to live as outlaws from the Word of the Lord. There is a great deal of difference between the cold callousness of a rebellious heart and the deeply troubled heart of a sincere Christian whose desperate prayer is "God save me from myself."

REMOVING THE CRUTCH

We don't confront what's wrong, we comfort what's wrong. Accept who you are and where you are before you move on. Not being who God wants you to be is like a train waiting to crash. Why do some of us go to church and worship God, return home and be evil, nasty and disrespectful to the ones we love? We need to wake up and get back into the rhythm of doing God's work. You will never win if you don't confront the obvious.

God didn't promise you a convenient life. He did not have a convenient life. God will make a way for you, but you have to provide the faith – faith in God will allow you to move mountains. Some of the people you are carrying, you need to turn them over to Jesus. You can't carry the load any longer. Those people are definitely holding you back. That's called a ball and chain. "LET THEM GO!"

I remember before I retired, there was a particular young lady who would borrow money from me every week. She would always pay me back on time. I became a crutch for her, I felt she had become a ball and chain for me. This particular day, I was determined to put a stop to this ordeal. I asked her: "Why do you borrow money from me every week?" She said because her money wasn't enough to go from one week to the next. I did not take her answer lightly, but I stopped loaning her money. She became so dependent on me. I began praying for her, asking God to show her how to manage her funds. Sometimes, you have to stop being a crutch and let people fend for themselves.

Why are we so afraid to be vulnerable? Is it fear? So what if you are vulnerable? When you are vulnerable, it brings on compassion and you leave yourself open to learning more. You become more approachable. Stop trying to protect your vulnerabilities. The past teaches us to hide our pain. Don't live a tasteless dead life. You will miss the love and joy waiting for you. Why reach for something that's in your hand. God gave us all we need to get our life in order. You should be rejoicing and praising God for every moment you can move your body and use your mind. Stop fighting God. He's not the enemy, He's on your side. God straightens and leads you to become a better you. There is nothing in your past that controls your destiny. God will teach you things you cannot see. When you are sick, even though there are billions of people in the world, God reaches out to help you. Just think – how can you not love a God so powerful who hears your call and comes to your aid. People, I say this again and again – trust God, He is the most powerful, loving, understanding, caring spirit you will ever encounter. I dare you to trust Him, once you give your life to God, you will not turn back to any of your old ways. Give it up – it's time. God's love has no limits.

TRUST JESUS IN THE GOOD AND BAD TIMES

Sometimes, in your life, money will not help you but the trust you put in God will conquer all. Some people will tell you different things about money – money is the root of all evil, or money is not everything. It's not the money, it's the person who's handling it. When you lean on God and don't try to sidestep Him, God's plan is bigger and better than you can ever imagine. Your character can get you places that your ability can't take you. God loves for you to trust Him. He wants you to lean on Him in good times and bad. Our grandparents got it right, they said, "Child trust in Jesus. He will carry you through."

Do you believe lazy people have financial problems? Underhand preparation will not last. Quick fix wealth does not work. None of this will last. Why not trust God with your finances? God is the only one who knows what your financial future looks like. What if you could read what God has planned for you? I think it would blow your mind. It's one thing to be on the ground, but it's another thing to fall to the ground. Once you are on the high road, do all you can to stay in God's grace, it's a long and hard fall from that mountain you have worked so hard to climb. Stay true to God, read His Word and treat people with respect.

Give God the honor He deserves, so you can keep what you have worked so hard to attain. Get to know God and how much you need to depend on Him. Knowing brings you into being. Have you noticed the closer you get to God, Satan steps in and tries to detour the promises God has for you? Your relationship with God depends on you staying healthy and happy. Don't sell yourself short for something that may look better than what God has to offer. Only believing and serving God will open up the gates of heaven. Every believer can hear from God. The Holy Spirit has been put in you. Use Him as a light to guide you to God. If you are seeking status to find yourself, you will not be found.

Seek peace and you can be rich even while you are broke. Woman you are loose, you are not waiting on God – God is waiting on you. Reading the Word each day can change your life. Reading and living the Word can change your journey. Look for ways to please God on a higher level than yourself. Every believer can hear from God. It can get a little scary if that happens, dial God's number and let Him be the judge. God can be a little misleading sometimes. Never fear, trust Him, He knows all. Stop being afraid of your circumstances. Challenge your bondage head on.

IN SPITE OF THE PAIN, FOLLOW THE WILL OF GOD

God has your hand, walk with Him. Act like you move in the spirit. The goal is to see yourself standing up praising God. When you let your enemies see what God has done for you – you might see a change in them. Have you ever been in transition when God wants you to change your ways? God will prepare you to go through some stuff that you would think is truly unreal. Your friends will think you are strange or different, but you know the change has to be made. God will push you from that environment in order to serve Him and make your life more tolerable. It's just like birthing. He pushes you from childhood to adulthood. Every so often, you may find yourself in a world that's too small. Sometimes, in life, you have to re-invent yourself – this can be traumatizing. The glory of God will contact your spirit to make a change in your life. Be ready to move in a split second. Don't put it off, waiting will jeopardize your blessing.

Can you relate to unconditional pain? Your pain has a perfect fit in your life. This is a part of God's plan God doesn't make mistakes. The key is what you do in the midst of pain. You can be bitter or better. Just go through it and grow through it. The enemy may turn on the heat, but God is in charge of the thermostat. God will not let anything defeat you. Every struggle makes you stronger. Don't complain about the pain. The pain prepares you for the future. Difficulties are part of life. You can take it. Healing comes when you take your mind off yourself. Don't feel defeated you are in the hands of the Almighty. God will make a way when you don't see a way. Everything happens for a reason. Can God trust you with the pain? We all have something to give; look for ways to stay in tune with God. God has shifted things in your direction. Stay encouraged, keep your head up and follow His will.

God did not build you to break you. You will bend, but not crumble. The power of who you are is based on what you think. Get rid of the negative thinking, God said, "fret not yourself." He is not through with you yet. When you have come through one of the worst years of your life, you have to shine this time around. When you realize you are unstoppable and you have God directing your steps, make no mistake, you are serving God immensely. Your season is here and now. This is your time to praise the Lord, rejoice and dance all over this land.

We all know when the devil is trying to raise hell, but he cannot compete with God. If you are one of God's anointed that means hands off. You are covered. When you are sleeping, the devil is working overtime to wreck your life and tear your dreams apart. Don't let go of God's hand. It is imperative that you and I take a stand against the devils of the world. We must read our Bibles and act on God's Word. Our lives belong to the Almighty, everyone has a role to play in this world. Your future targets your wellbeing. If you want to live a peaceful life, be patient and wait on God. There is no greater gift than knowing God, and serving Him. Be careful how you carry yourself, God is always watching. God never forgets a labor of love or the ministry He provides for you. Perhaps, you may have helped someone on their way to success, and they walk away not thinking about you. Not to worry, you have obeyed God.

TAKE HOLD OF GOD'S PROMISES

Isn't it strange how we pursue God, and not be prepared to confront obstacles? We must face our fears and survive the stares of our peers who either do not approve of who we have become or sneer at us because of who we once were. If we are going to reach our goals in Christ or in life, we must press through public opinion and intimidation. Do you realize every step we take is moving us closer and closer to our destiny? The bitter taste of fear is neutralized by the sweet expectation of victory! Those of you who think that excellence has escaped you – that virtue has vanished – it is time to change your mind. To those who simply survive by flipping the pages of your calendar without living your life, I say – there is more. To those who are coasting comfortably through this present season – there is always room for improvement. Whatever your situation, I invite you to come, join me for a journey through Proverbs 31 and see the kind of woman God has ordained you to be.

I want God to use me as his instrument to get the word to his people and learn the principles of God's gifts. God's favors are yours. We need to know what He is asking us in order to deliver to His people. How have you experienced God's goodness? God's favor is on your side. Faith, power, and grace are always at hand. Whenever God is trying to take you somewhere, this my people is called birthing. It becomes a new beginning in your life. Prepare yourself for the road, it's about to get a little bumpy.

Transition will tap into your mind. Take hold of the promises of God and ride that problem until you are satisfied with the outcome. If you have to start a new life, that's OK. You will find that this is a rebirth of a new beginning. Learn to accept change because as long as you live, there will be changes in your life one after another. When you are in transition, you cannot control it. Just keep moving and stay positive holding on to God's unchanging hands. God will get you to your destiny. Stay encouraged, you are in transition to become something great.

Life has its own consequences, you will be surprised when you get to heaven and see some of the people you thought should not be there. Ask yourself this – How did you get there? You did the same thing those people did. You asked

God to forgive you for your sins. This is not about you; it's about how you impact someone's life. God will use you to flow grace into somebody else's life. When you are willing to let God use you to be a blessing to somebody, God will bless you. Be an instrument of God, make it about serving Him. Let God use your hands to extend to someone, may it be a hug or a handshake. If you are a God fearing person, God's goodness will flow from you into the person you lay your hands on. That's being an instrument of God. Use every available tactic to bring souls to Him. Learn to love, and appreciate God for using you. Work the mind God gave you. He called you through grace, not through works. We have to demonstrate God's love to others. Pray for our president, mayors, and all government officials that they will learn more about God, and not rely on their own understandings.

■   ■   ■

Chapter 7

Becoming All God Wants You to Be

The Bible is full of wonderful people! I have written about some of them and have learned powerful lessons for my life from their lives. Some people never find their reason for living until their later years. Until you find your purpose, you will want to roll over and die. But if you give into temptation, you would have stopped short of God's restoration. You would have gone to your grave never knowing what blessing God was about to pour out for you. You would have died in bitterness without having tasted His joy. So take courage, if no one comes to assist you, pick yourself up and walk on. Walk right pass the agony people inflicted and listen for the Word of God. It will come. You may not be delivered by a human hand. It will be the hand of Jesus.

I remember as a small child about four years old playing in the front yard where white sand covered the entire yard. I made up this song:

Doodle Bug
© Joanne Carter

Doodle bug, Doodle bug come out to play.
I need a friend today.
Send your friends and God will say,
Tell Joanne she is here to stay.

That song still resonates in me today. I knew nothing about God, only what I heard from my parents. As I look back, I can see God's hands on my life. We all know how meaningful and precious loving God is in our lives. God's love for me is priceless.

It is vital that you do good and not evil. Do not trust malicious people. If there is evil in their hearts, it is time to be cleansed. Evil often results from unresolved hurt and bitterness that has become infected and left to fester in the human heart. Jesus is the healer of hurts. He is able to turn even the hardest, most evil hearts into a garden of love and grace. Look for ways to be good to people. Encourage people in hard places, talk less and listen longer. When you give your heart to help and pray with others, God will give you the ability and the compassion to show others how to step out on faith.

Take the test of the "haves" and the "have-nots." See where your faith lies. Has God answered your prayers in every area of your life? Having it all and making it big in this life does not get you to heaven; your love and faith in God will open the gates of heaven. Be aware of how you live, take nothing for granted; be the most God-fearing person you can possibly be. In the eyes of God, you are His most prized possession. He made you, He can prosper you. God hears your cry. He will protect you from all that comes before you. Be serious about your belief in God. Humble yourself and look to Him for all your beginnings.

GETTING ON TRACK

Are you blaming yourself for things you cannot control? We have to move barriers to get our destinies on track. Is there a reason people don't like you, or you don't like them? Test your system: could it be you're not understanding them or is it your response to others. Your system may be blocking your blessings. Maybe you need to grow up and challenge yourself in a mature manner. Identify this system every time it shows up. Don't lose your chance to advance by holding on to it. Put away this childish behavior. Don't defend something that is killing you. Look at how long you have been on this earth – what have you accomplished?

Have you accomplished all God has planned for you? Stop following people, you should be leading. Kill the system. You cannot put away what you cannot identify. If you resist it, it will flee. Don't give the forbidden system strength. Change your outlook, change your thinking; put those childish ways out of your life and become the adult God wants you to be. God guides and nurtures us to be His voice in order to bring souls to Him. God will not push us into doing things He has not equipped us to do. Isn't it strange how we argue with ourselves when God wants us to be who He wants us to be? But our concept of God comes from our upbringing. We need to recognize our place in this world. We sit around thinking of childish things   how to plot revenge, and how to tell people off. Do you realize you are destroying your chance to become a model for others to follow? Your children, friends, and relatives are looking for a way of living a godly life. Wake up people! Life is a script you are on stage. Everybody is watching you. Save the children who are sitting around not being productive. Those children need to be like Bill Gates looking for their greatness. Parents, churches, show our children the way. They deserve to have greatness in their lives. Learn to be thankful for the children of our future. Believe it or not, we are on our way out. Let's teach our children the rights of the world. The Bible leads our children to God. Let's sow this information and our experiences into our children. Today is the day! Our children are our future, teach them well, and let them lead the way.

ARISE! YOU ARE NEVER ALONE

Do you know when you are alone, it's a test of your character. Living for Christ is a challenge. It tests your faith; however, the experience you receive is rewarding. I believe our purpose is to give back, do better and be a great teacher to our children; help our children to persevere, become great achievers, take nothing for granted, and stand on the shoulders of our great leaders. They must dream big, love their crafts, and put all their faith in the Alpha and the Omega.

There is nothing quite as frightening for a person than to walk into a room full of self-righteous people. It's like a woman of today walking through gunfire with no bullet-proof vest. Have you ever stepped into a house and found yourself the object of a room full of unwelcoming stares – no one even says hello? When you focus on Jesus all fears vanish. Just one look into the warm eyes of a loving Savior can disarm everything life uses to assault our peace. Can you imagine Him in the room with you? Just knowing He is there clearly dispels any apprehensions you may have felt and comforts you in His wonderful presence. Though it sometimes happens in a public place, when we recognize the presence of God, we are immediately alone with Him – that is the most glorious place we can be. And so it is with all who love Him. We give Him public praise for the private things He has done for us. It is the secret things He has done that make us all weep at His feet.

I feel a resurrection coming to the distraught heart of empty women who have poured themselves out over and over. This is the time for you to arise. If you have become a martyr to your marriage – arise! If you have been a minister to your children – arise! If you are burned out, stressed out, laid out, cold, and lifeless – arise! Expect God to show up and raise you up again. God is not through with you yet. He has a plan and purpose for your life. And though you may be tired, weak, and weary, it is not over until God says it's over. My people, put death on hold and drive depression out, for the word of the Lord comes to those who has given too much to everyone else. The Lord says, "Today is your day. ARISE!"

THE LANGUAGE OF MARRIAGE

Let me speak on marriages. I've been married twice. I know a little about the language of marriage. Have you ever noticed that men and women sometimes seem to be speaking different languages? Women tend to be verbal while men tend to be physical. Women want to talk about everything – men don't always use words. Even male-to-male, men often communicate through touch. A pat on the back means "I like you." A coach's playful slap on a basketball player's rump says, "Good job!"

Men and women need to learn each other's language. As a man, whenever you feel affectionate, you want to buy her flowers. As women, we go wild over a card. The first few years of your marriage is about learning each other's language. Ask your spouse why she or he does what they do and say what they say. Better yet, begin to observe their method of communication. You do not want to live in a tower of BABEL. That's the place where families became divided because they could not understand each other's languages. You had better get busy and learn before frustration turns your household into BABEL! At Babel, all progress ceases and confusion takes over.

When approaching your spouse, don't corner the person. No one wants to feel interrogated. You may be surprised that men tend to avoid open confrontation. I've seen macho men intimidated by one hundred pound women. The Bible says...

> It is better to live in a corner of a roof Than in a house shared with a contentious woman. (Proverbs 25:24 NASB)

Remember, you can win the argument and lose the man. Everything you were going to do for him when he changes, do it now and do it by faith. I pray that God would interpret the language of your love so that your marriage will be powerful and productive.

A NEW ATTITUDE

When you do what's right, God will never leave you without guidance. Don't copy what's in front of you, be original. Don't lease your grace out to the world and let them call it talent. Grace is Jesus in us, the hope of glory. God has a strategy for our lives. Our future has already been laid out for us. Follow

God's plan, walk that chalk line, you have the power of agreement on your life. If you don't recognize your walk with God, you will be left without a plan. Your destiny is already in you. Put away the old system of doing things. Don't defend things that are not of God. Watch what you say, don't poison your life by speaking ill of yourself. God said that in all your getting, you should get understanding.

Take a serious stand, stay in the jet stream of life. Don't go against the flow. Draw in defeat, you control the door to your mind. Keep your mind filled with good thoughts. Draw in the good faith of God. The battle is in your mind. Start speaking positives as opposed to negatives. Give yourself permission to strive for the best. Put a pep in your step, have a fresh new attitude, choose to be happy. Be determined to be good to somebody. Get up, open your window and declare happiness over your life. The God we serve is well able to give us all we need.

In life, you will be afraid sometimes, but keep the faith, God is not far from you. Your battles will never be bigger than God. Keep your mind on Him. God's greatest pleasure is to know you trust Him. When you re-knew your mind, it causes your spirit to resonate so deep into your soul, you cannot do anything but trust God. You want to work toward pleasing God. He will give you supernatural gifts to renew the spirit of your mind. He cares for you.

When the brook dries up. What will you do? You've lost your job, your wife has left you, your children are gone, and you are on the verge of losing your mind. Trust God – give Him all of you. God doesn't ask for much. You know about the mustard seed. God is telling you what to ask for. Use your God-given educated mind, come off your high horse and worship Him. Do as He asks, God will make your life an abundance of joy and peace. Who in this world wouldn't want that? People, listen to me: When God comes for you, be ready. Line your life up with His will. Not your will, but His will. Let it be said, let it be written, and let it be done.

MARY'S STORY

I grew up as a preacher's kid so I can talk about Jesus, give some encouraging words, sing songs, and so forth.

On July 5, 1995, is when I really knew Jesus had entered into my heart, spirit, and mind. I went into the hospital for an ongoing procedure and ended up having to stay for a week. When I woke up, I was surrounded by family members. Some were crying and others looked sad. I was still drugged but peeping up asking what was wrong? The doctor and nurse came in to inform me about what had happened. I shed a few tears and went back to sleep. However, the next morning, I was told what happened and what needed to be done. Surprisingly, I understood what he was saying. I felt a calmness come over me. The doctor continued to explain my situation. I knew God was still in control. This was only a temporary setback.

After plenty of hospital visits, stays, and tears, I began to feel down. I wanted to know, why it was taking so long for me to healed. I lay on the floor of my bedroom and began to call on the name of Jesus. Crying, "Father, I stretch my hands to thee. Help me Jesus!" I remember getting up saying, "Thank you Jesus." I know my healing was on the way. YES! He led me, gave me strength, and I love Him because He is.

My family, loved ones and friends saw me through this. I also believe that I saw a change in the doctor's attitude. God continues to bless me every day. He heard my cry. As long as I live and trouble arises, I will hasten to His throne. What a mighty God I serve.

–Mary F. Morris

DESTINED TO WIN

You are destined to win but only if you follow God. Sometimes, we get frustrated and want to throw up our hands and say, "I can't do this anymore." Although we don't act on those feelings and we may think about quitting in order to let off steam – quitting is never an option. There are ways to solve problems and still be in control. Being a weakling in the spirit can cause you to be unprotected. Look for ways to motivate yourself. Haven't your parents told you never to be in a hurry to become an adult? Life can reduce you to a humble servant. Keep the faith, stay in prayer and stand with Jesus. Master where you are. Work it out and finish the course. Hold on the course you are pursuing, it will get worse before it gets better. Stay in your lane. Do not look left or right, forget about your past. Look forward and let the light of God lead you to the promised land.

Use the power God has given you. Throw away the thrones that are hindering you. Rise above your situation. Keep a pray at hand. Don't quit, the best is yet to come. Stand on the grounds of possessiveness. It's not how you live, it's how well you live. Many of us want promotion without process. If you follow God, He will take you to the next dimension. Your future is tied to your past.

Destiny will bring the future into full focus if you commit time and energy to the process. You cannot feed tomorrow, and neglect the present. Make a move toward doing what's right; your move is important to your future but remember, brick walls await you. You will be attacked by people who are seeking to gain control. Remember, when your life is in a rehearsal stage, don't expect a loud applause. Recognize your potential, be faithful to your beginning. Let God mold you into your potential. Keep on working on your level. Destiny will pull you into your greatness. Your gifts will come from the assignment God has for you. You cannot live in darkness; we serve a great God. He is with us to lead us, direct us, and help us to believe in ourselves. Every step you take has been ordered by God.

GOD WILL HONOR YOUR FAITH

How many times have you blown your blessing by not keeping your mouth closed? Don't give the devil an open door to trample over your life. The quieter you are, the more you can hear God talking to you. You have to know when to give a testimony and when not. Know the power of your words. Things need to be kept between you and God. James 3 chapter 3-5 speaks on the usage of the tongue. If you stop complaining and realize the tongue should not be used for gossip and negativity, you will find there are lots of subjects to engage in. Your words have the power to affect your life, job, and others. Your journey awaits you. Honor God because He has always given us great opportunities to be the best. Why not partner with God and see where He takes you. Regardless of your position or your past, God raises people equally. No matter how many mistakes you have made, it is your faith God honors. You may have blown it, but God is in the business of restoring broken lives and rebuilding homes. You may have been like Rahab, but if you can believe in God, He will save your house. Faith was there, God protected the faith-filled house.

Understand this one fact: if you have been treated unfairly, get up off the floor and take a seat at the master's table – you are worthy. You have the right to be in the place and position you are in, not because of your goodness, but by virtue of His invitation. I pray that God will heal your thoughts until you are able to enjoy and rest in what He is doing in your life right now! Nurturing a problem not only means you keep it, it also implies that you are feed-ing it. It is drawing your strength; just as an unborn child can only get food from his mother. The enemy cannot live in a blood-washed, regenerated spirit. The enemy can only thrive in your mind if you let him live off your old memo-ries and fears. He is a leech that relies upon your umbilical cord for survival. Cut that cord and watch your fears starve to death.

"Lord, there have been times when I have felt so different, so weird, so unlike the people I know. It has taken me a while to figure out that I am different by divine design. I am dif-ferent because you have made me with gifts and traits, a genetic combination that no one else has. No one in all the ages of the world has ever been me. And no one ever will be. So I celebrate the fact that you have made each tiny part of me unique, one of a kind. Deliver me, Father, from feel-ing weird. Deliver me from ever wishing I was someone else. Help me to enjoy the little things that make me special. Help me to understand what a rare and precious treasure I am to you. Help me to realize that I can give the world some things that no one else can give in the same way. Thank you, Lord for the awesome creative work you've done as you've made me who I am."

AMAZING WISDOM FROM MY MOTHER

I once had the privilege of entertaining my ninety-year-old mother, whose robust frame and bountiful body had deteriorated to just a mere shadow of its former presence. Her hair had turned to wisps reminding me of the angel hair we used to decorate our Christmas tree with when I was a child. Nevertheless, her spirit seemed strong and graceful. I saw the burning embers of a fire, embers of wisdom buried deep beneath the ashes of her experience. When I looked beyond her slow steps and brittle bones, I realized that she still passed more flame in her winter than most people muster in the heat of summer! I recognized her as a woman who had come to the setting of the sun. I could see the sun still burning beneath her leathery skin and brilliant eyes. It seemed that age had somehow smothered her need to talk. She would lapse into long periods of silence that left me clamoring foolishly through my own conversation. When asked if she was all right, she would assure me that she was greatly enjoying my company. Then she would flee again into the counsel of her own thoughts, coming out occasionally just to humor me.

As I pondered her demeanor, I realized that her silence did not indicate boredom. It was, first of all, the mark of someone who had learned how to be alone. Relatively telling me to relax and enjoy life. During that visit, I determined to understand two secrets of my mother's wisdom. First, I commit to renewing my faith and trust in the abode of God. Second, I promised to spend more time with myself, to warm myself at the fire of my own thoughts and smile with the contentment of the riches God has for me. I have fought a good fight and with God on my side, I have made it to where peace, joy, and happiness reside.

GOD IS ALWAYS A STEP AHEAD

People, I know it will take a lot to stand strong. But it is worth it. When you can see the goodness of God, isn't it worth the effort to do His will, so you can reach that happy median? Let's live our lives for the glory of God. I was taught that trying was of utmost importance. So I was afraid not to try. As a result, I boldly tried God, His mercy endures forever.

When you wait on God, only the best will come. I have a friend who is like how most of us were in our younger days – doing everything our way. She waited on God for quite some time. Isn't it strange how God answers our prayers in the midst of nowhere? God is a way-maker and a heart regulator in His own time. He knows when you are ready because He prepares you without your knowledge. He blesses you with the people who are suited for His purpose.

My friend Ann Missouri Crowder has gone home to glory. One day, in particular, she stayed on my mind, so I decided to call her. When I did, a child answered. I asked for Ann, the child gave the phone to Ann's husband or so I thought. He proceeded to tell me they had been divorced for seven years. She became ill and passed away in 2013. I said a silent prayer, and whispered, "you will be missed." The hurt still lingers. In the seventies, Stanley, Ann, Samuel and I were married at that time. We were always out together. Ann became my daughter's god-mother. Isn't it strange how you just move on and lose touch? When God wants you to embark on other interests, you will not stay in the same circle. No one is rooted or beholden to each other forever.

I remember the four of us, Stanley, Ann, Sam and I attended a beach party. I got into the water at a level that was deeper than I thought. I went under once, I lost control and went under the second time. Stanley spotted me and knew I was in trouble. He swam over and pulled me up as I was going under for the third time. I was frightened. I'm not sure if I could ever thank him enough. I thank God for him being in the right place at the right time. Stanley literally saved my life. God truly had His hand on me because He had something for me to accomplish. I will always be at His mercy. He is not through with me yet.

What I know for myself is God can be trusted. No matter how many problems are circling our lives, God is always steps ahead. The Word works! Greater is He that is in me than he that's in the world. Your labor is not in vain. Hang in there, keep believing, keep seeking, keeping praying, you have a crown waiting for you. With all the issues, heartaches, doubts, fears, anxieties, promises – people, you have a story to tell. Remember, God did some amazing things with Moses. When you challenge a person to come out of their familiar into their unfamiliar, they aren't always nice. God wants to bring you out of your comfortable place, so He can move you to a higher plane. God inspires people the way He inspired Moses. You will never see Him create discord. Everything is original with God. Remember, no two fingerprints are alike. You are who God intended for you to be. He put genes in you to become who He wants you to be. Your talents are locked inside of you until God is ready to bring them out. I call them destiny genes. These genes are lying dormant waiting for the word from God. Sometimes, in your life, you will meet people who don't believe in your dreams. Don't get concerned, let your dreams leap in the direction God wants them to go. Don't die with your dreams locked inside of you.

■   ■   ■

Chapter 8

Victory is Yours

D o you argue with God? Knowing you can't win. No one can outshine God. Please don't put yourself in a delusional state. Open your Bible and read about the people who try to outshine God. You will find out how God handles His business. The problem with the world is – we don't live up to responsibilities. We cannot change anything unless we band together. Put God first and plead your case.

If you do what you want and not follow God you will suffer the consequences. God holds the key to your future. God sets the boundaries. God respects the person He created. Be honorable enough to make a decision to partner with God. Many times, we will go through periods of being angry with God. It's ok, God understands we are human. But here is the thing. If we don't understand what's going on in our lives, we have the tendency to blame God or someone else. If you would stop, and calm yourself, God will speak to your spirit and give you the next step to overcome the problems you are dealing with. When you lose touch with God, you open up the windows for Satan to step in. People of God that's not good. Be a sergeant for the Almighty. After all, what would you do without His guidance? God has given all of us gifts – you have a mind which is so powerful when it's put to good use. Everything we have comes from God. God wants us to use our tools to glorify Him. In return, God takes care of all our needs and wants. Knowing that there is a God closer than any brother or sister is comforting. Just open your heart and mind – let Him in. He will not force His will on you. God is patient, loving, reliable, and absolutely the greatest.

GOD OF CHANGE

God knows how to take a mess and turn it into a miracle. If you're in a mess, don't be upset because God specializes in cleaning up messes. God is saying some definite things about people being set free and delivered to fulfill their purpose in the kingdom. When the Lord gets through working on you, all your adversities will be put to shame. Your accusers and all the people who contributed to your low self-esteem will have to admit they were wrong.

Many people have not seen Jesus as the answer to their dilemma. They go to church, love the Lord, and they want to go to heaven. But they still don't see Him as the solution to their problems. We may seek help by going from one person to another, but only Jesus is the answer. You can't spend the rest of your life trying to protect yourself from the struggles of life. You will have to face economical, spiritual or sociological persuasion! If you become intimidated by that fact, it will cause you to live your life in an emotional incubator – insulated but isolated. Having declared that, we must no longer focus on protecting ourselves, but we must be willing to love and to risk and to dare. Where there is no passion, there is no power.

The enemy will attempt either to steal your passion or to smother it beneath the fear of failure and rejection. Without passion, you will become passive and unable to achieve the purpose of God in your life.

Change is not always an enemy. It can be God's way of saying enough is enough. He will promote you from one task to another, if you can remain flexible and face the changes of life with the assurance of God, you will win. It is God's desire to make you a wiser person. What I am trying to tell you is – life has a middle name, and the name is change. Anything that grows will change. No two days will be the same. They were not designed to be duplicated. Each one is a new expression of a multifaceted God whose being cannot be defined in just one circumstance. Each day, we will behold a new wonder of His glory. You get to rejoice in a day that someone else missed – while you slept someone gasped a final sigh and slipped from time into eternity without seeing this day. But you are still here. This is God's gift to you – enjoy it. Change will come soon enough.

FROM VICTIM TO VICTORY

The secret of being transformed from a vulnerable victim to a victorious, loving person is found in the ability to open your past to someone responsible enough to share your weaknesses and pain. There can be no better first step toward deliverance than to find a Christian counselor or pastor, and come out of hiding. If you seek God's guidance and the help of competent leadership, you will find someone who can help you work through your pain and suffering. The church is a body. No one operates independently of another. We are all in this together.

You know, what really excites me is knowing that I'm not going to HELL.

A LETTER TO GOD FROM THE HOMELESS

"Lord, you are the God of my desert and all my dry places. I'm stuck here again in the wilderness helpless, hopeless, and friendless, with no home for my heart. It's a desperate, desolate place. I have visited this wide wasteland before, feeling trapped between where I am and where I want to be. Like the children of Israel, I am wondering and wondering if I will ever get out of here? Is there even a place beyond this pain? It's not that I don't know how to put one foot in front of the other. It's that I want to be where I am not. I need the God of fire by night and cloud by day. I need direction from the maker of the stars. There's a promised land before me, a place of provision, a place of plenty. But how do I exchange my emptiness for your abundance? I want to go forward with you. Lord, lead me home."

Most Christians are seated so high on their perch of self-righteousness that they often fail to minister to the pain behind the sin. They are concerned about the habits of sin. But they don't seem to understand that removing the act doesn't free the heart. It just represses a problem that manifests in cynicism and frustration. People are teachable when they are not in pain. It is like telling a child not to scratch a rash – she will do it even if she is feeling discomfort. But if you can apply a soothing ointment, the habit is easily broken. Because of the good things He wants to send you, God wants to heal every fear, insecurity, and inhibition that would stop you from receiving what is yours. Use the power of a request when you ask for your blessing. When it comes, be ready for a downpour.

LIFE HAS A RHYTHM

Does an individual go to hell because they sin? Or do they go to hell because they don't have faith in God? We are God's instruments. God uses His faithful people to bring souls closer to Him. Why do you think God asks us to be radical about our "solicitudes". Solicitudes are those things that we are anxious or concerned about. God cares about us. He loves you too much to see you twisted with pain because of something you should have cast away a long time ago. God has no problem making that thing leave you alone. The struggle is getting you to lose your grip on it. He speaks to you, not the thing bothering you. He tells you to get rid of it. Can you do it? Yes! But you have to play your part; that part is faith. God's promises cannot be earned or merited. They come only through faith. "By faith" we understand that the worlds were framed by the Word of God so that the things which are seen were not made of things which are visible. God wants us to understand that just because we can't see it, doesn't mean He won't do it. We can be delivered. However, we are not free because some of that stuff still controls us. Now is the time to set things straight. God has assembled our bodies to carry out His work.

People, we have a pulse. Energy is the key. If the people you are around don't have the same pulse, it kills your productivity. We have to walk together and keep the rhythm going. Have you been living without a rhythm? You have everything you need on the outside, but you can't fit into anyone's rhythm. This is your year, pick-up the pace.

Many years ago, I worked as a scamstress at a well-known manufacturing company. In order to keep up and to achieve productivity, there had to be a rhythm of progress. The same applies to everyday life. Watch yourself when walking with God. Stay in your lane. Put yourself in the presence of others who are greatness bound. People who can give you the push you need will be a complement to your future. Take the flight and fly into your destiny. God is standing by to direct your life, change your ways and your mind. God is your only resource. Keep up with Him, He has the rhythm.

DON'T BOW TO SATAN

The principle is that every person has a philosophy. Take off the lenses of the world and put on the lenses of God. You need to see the world as God sees it. He not only wants us to have what we need, He wants us to have desires and abundance in life.

People criticize Creflo Dollar for buying a new plane and for asking his congregation to take part in purchasing it. The plane he had at the time had faults, which put his family in danger. This preacher is on a mission for God. His schedule is phenomenal. He has to travel to different countries and cities, I'm sure he needs reliable transportation.

Pastor Dollar is spreading the gospel of grace around the world. That's his assignment from God. If you believe in God and the promises and assignments He has given you, He will rock your world. Rise up, God has chosen you to see through the lenses of the world. At the end of time, we will all have to answer to a higher power.

Giving an extended hand should never be controlled. Learn to give freely. Give support to the kingdom. Remember favor is on your side.

God gave me leadership in what He wanted me to do. We are bound with drugs, and alcohol; our children are running wild, not being loved, hurting others and themselves. They are killing and bound up with hatred, fatherless and motherless. Babies are having babies, men are abandoning their responsibilities and children are being beaten and thrown away. Children are becoming prostitutes, girls are selling their bodies, fathers are molesting their children, people are going hungry. There is homelessness and older people are left to fend for themselves. There is no peace, no joy, no love, and no one to care. God where are you? God what's going on? Tell the devil to let your people go. Men are marrying men, women are marrying women; there is fornication, and people are worshiping money and objects – God, please, tell Satan to let your people go. We are knocking on your door, please let your people in. Tell us what to do. Lead your people out of this bondage. God, the burden is too heavy. Free us God! We are sinking in sin. Let us hide in thee. What the Devil meant for evil, God will turn it around and make it good. The waters may seem deep, but God will never let you drown. God knows you have been down too long. He will comfort you. He's there to meet your every need. God promised you, He will be your bright and shining star. Follow Him, let your heart be free. From the pit of your sins, God rescued you. God is the Bread of Life. He will not let you lose your way. Take God's hand and walk with Him, Jesus has what it takes to meet your needs. The message of the cross is there for you every waking moment.

Do the people of this world recognize that the devil plays a significant role in their lives? Do you know the Lord plays a part in this world as well? God does not inflict harm upon His people. God's love for us is relentless. God will pull you out of any ditch. He will show up to put your mind at ease. He will not rejoice over our mishaps, He's not out to get you. God will take everything you went through to teach you to be strong enough to go through all He has in store for you. Walk in God's light. Walk through and say a pray.

This is the time you need to reach down and use what God has put in you. If God redeemed you before, He will do it again. You will have an abundance of great fullness. You are under the Shepherd's watch. If you can, praise Him when you are hungry, lonely, and tired – give Him your all. When you are under attack, your blessings are on the way. Only bow down to God, never to Satan.

God has opened the door, it's open for you. Make Jesus the number one in your life. Learn to live the way Jesus lived. Loving people, respecting yourself. Be free from the world. God's mission is to save souls. Get the whole package, the time is now. This is the season when God isn't saying anything. God wants you to reach down in your spirit and pull out what He has already fed you.

Nancy Reagan said, "just say no!" You must say no to your flesh. In order to be disciplined to the Word of God. The flesh wants what it wants, but God knows what you need. What do you do when the Devil is talking and God is saying nothing? This is exactly the way God wants us to react. Satan uses the same method on people that he used on Eve. Eve bit, and Adam followed. People are defeated because they forget how to fight. If you apply God's method to your life, there is no way you can lose. There is a difference between knowing your path and walking your path. Don't let your situation take you into darkness – it could be deadly.

Where there is a blessing, make no mistake, there is a battle. Do not evacuate the territory you possess. Stand on what you know, not what you feel. Why are we loyal to things that do not work? Is the Devil keeping our heads in a fog? Why are we not able to recognize what the devil is doing? He is messing with our heads to keep us in the dark. Let's put our heads together and shift this thing. Keep a level head in the midst of the battle. Your life will be better. If you will surrender to God, you will see miracles working in your life. Set your attitude in a positive position. You hold the faith, allow God to do the work. Experience God's best, grace moves on your behalf. Let's empower each other to change the negatives to positives, and follow the Word of God. When you pray and believe you will have what you desire. Operate through the Spirit – that's everlasting. If you operate through flesh – that's corruption.

FACING REJECTION

If you were abused as a child, you grow up with more problems than the pain of the abuser. You also live with the anger that nobody helped you. Nobody intervened on your behalf, nobody stepped in and rescued you. People may have seen, but nobody helped. God said something like this, "You were cast out into the open field and everybody loathed you." That's the way people feel if they were abused as a child. Like a thrown away baby. But abused women aren't the only ones who feel this way. Divorced women, rejected women, and abandoned women feel this way too. In fact, virtually every person goes through this experience at some time.

When people reject you, it's very difficult for you to feel good about yourself. You start thinking, you are not worthy. I beg you not to allow another person's view of you to control the way you see yourself. That's too much power to give to another human being. Recognize that those who reject you have no ability to see the inside of you. Refuse to accept the loathing of other people. Don't allow their opinions to creep into your inner person. If no one else has compassion for you, remember, God does and that's reason enough to be good to yourself.

"Lord, I cannot even articulate everything I need from you. I have to rest in the promise that you know my every need and that you will provide. Send your Holy Spirit to minister to every aspect of this situation to bring truth, to bring wisdom, to bring redemption, and to bring a vision of what to do next. As I said, there is nothing left but you, and you are all I need. You are my rock, my one stable place, my only sure foundation."

YOUR BLESSINGS WILL COME

Let me tell you the way things work for me. Just before my seed springs forth, just before my miracle happens, just before my promise is fulfilled, that's when all hell seems to break out against me. Just before I experience the fullness of God's power working in me, that's when the Devil tries to break me. But while I'm waiting, all the makings of a miracle are growing inside of me.

Before I wrote a book. I wrote a letter to myself. I told myself you can make it, don't give up. You have gone through too much to die now. You may cry, but you will not die. There's got to be something else for you. There's got to be a reason you feel the way you feel. There's got to be a blessing on its way. These are the words I believe the Lord wants me to say to all of you. Don't die! Keep standing! God is about to give you another seed to birth. He is about to open up the windows of heaven and pour you out a blessing that's so great you won't have room enough to receive it. When God restores you, you will suddenly walk in a different light. Your life will no longer be in the dark. You are now moving into your destiny. Your past is behind you, your future is facing you, get busy and collect your blessings. You don't have time to think about the past.

You will be so busy living in your blessings that all the former things in your life will be out of sight and out of mind. You will finally be free. What doesn't kill you will make you stronger.

Isn't it strange how letting go is especially painful when you allow your relationship with your child to become cluttered like an attic stuffed with things that belong somewhere else? Often, there are misplaced passions dumped on the child to compensate for loneliness in other areas. Because there was no place to put them, they were shoved into the attic. Often, it is love that should have been invested in a spouse, but there was no spouse or no capacity in the spouse to love. So the love was dumped on a child. This is not a healthy love, it is obsessive. Every good mother, sooner or later, must understand she is denied ownership; she is merely granted stewardship. This is the understanding you need to mother God's children, God's way. But understand this: The Lord steps in when the devil thinks He is winning. Keep the faith, if you're going to see your dreams come to pass. If you're going to see those promises fulfilled, you have to focus on the positive. The good news is that God never runs out of options. He has the final say.

Don't ponder any situation. Visit it and discard it. Stay in tune to what you want your world to be. When you get your direction, God will be your compass.

When times get tough, get closer to God. The enemy cannot stop what God has for you. Don't settle for mediocrity. Don't give up on yourself. God is standing by waiting for you to lean on Him. When you see your health and your circumstances get better, you will know God has shown up to rescue you. Ask Him to touch you again and again, and keep it moving. It can be done.

■   ■   ■

Chapter 9

God Is on Your Side

Jesus knew He was a new creation. This world changed when God gave His only Son to die as a sacrifice for our sins. God will give you power to change, to be a new creation, if only you believe in Him. People, it's time for new things – Jesus has been certified to be a brilliant leader. This is more than a position. The devil will still beat up on you just because you want to get right with Jesus. Don't you know the flesh will defeat you? Your emotions will take over. However, there is a solution, the Spirit *is* in you, not on you. God will always have something up His sleeve. God has the keys to unlock every door in your life. We've seen God's goodness, and we are thankful. But let's get serious – God is not satisfied because He wants to make you better. It's called a second touch, get in agreement with God. Declare success over your life. He controls the universe and when your enemies come against you, they know that He has something in store for you. God can do the impossible, you don't have to be strong all the time, even Jesus fell down carrying the cross. Jesus knew we will be weak at times. That's why He is always there for you. Settle down, wait on God. He is always there to control every moment.

Now that you have this information, you should share it. If you are a child of God, you should have the power of God to motivate and lead others to the cross. You are not here to manipulate anyone; you are here to have a relationship with God. You are not here to take; you are here to give. Get in the battle and take what is rightfully yours. You are now in a spiritual warfare. Be careful now; you are tramping on dangerous ground and you cannot be a weakling. Stand strong because the devil is waiting at the door to take you down. Move that stumbling block out of your path. When God steps in, confronts the devil and says: "This is my child let her be!" Your miserable days are over. God has made you His priority. You are now on your way to greater things.

HOOK-UP–DON'T LOOK BACK

Get the holy hook-up, and don't look back. When you believe your sins have been forgiven, the healing has already begun. God will not burden you with rules and regulations. So don't be dismayed. God will spend time with you because He wants you to live the life of freedom. Giving honor to Him on all levels. The fact that God has endowed you with ability proves that He has a purpose for you. He gave you the gifting, but you will have to give an account of what you did with it. Every day is a gift from God. What you do with that day or with your talent is up to you, but it's your gift from God. Have you ever hidden your talent because someone said you didn't have it? You are only limited by your own creativity and concentration. You need to exercise your potential. Get your blood circulating! Good spiritual aerobic exercises will start your heart pumping. A stimulating life can even help guard you against mischief and sin. When you're bored, Satan takes the initiative. Are you aware where that will lead you?

It's possible to construct an obstacle in your mind. Don't be limited by your own tendency to settle for less. If you're not careful, you will talk yourself out of living. Speak up and say, "I need more life in my life!" Is it hard to believe you can be loved when you are not needed? The truth of the matter is, the need is still there but the areas of need have changed. You must be wise, if not, you create a cold war that will leave you alone with bitterness and sad memories. Hostility will cause you to be left with Thanksgiving turkey to eat by yourself. It is not worth it, with wisdom, grace, and prayer, you can enjoy it all the days of your life.

I remember in my early modeling days, so far away from home. I could visualize the Thanksgiving dinner. As I sat there, I thought about the fact that my greatest blessings of life cannot be bought. Communication happens in unexpected ways between people who do not need audible speech. The language is a quick glance or a soft pat on the shoulder. The communication is a concerned look when all is not well. This is the wealth that causes street people to smile in the rain and laugh at a storm. If you already have a covenant friend, savor your days together. If you don't have such a friend, ask God, the covenant-maker to send you a partner of the heart. The Lord said He will dwell in the dark cloud.

> I have surely built you an exalted house, and place for you to dwell in forever. (1 Kings 8:13 NKJV)

Has anyone ever called you a "cry baby" Are you so convinced that your life could be different that you are willing to stagger to the altar and pray while others are playing? Do you want something from God so much that you are willing to risk the opinions of those who accuse you of being too emotional in the way you ask God for it? Do you believe so passionately that you are intoxicated with the hope of what God has for you? What dream consumes your thinking, your feelings, your believing? Pray about that, because if your prayer request doesn't move you, it probably won't move God.

Use your troubles to free your passion. When your troubles are great enough and your desires are strong enough, you will feel that you have nothing to lose and everything to gain by pouring out all your passion before Him. Don't allow yourself to be intimidated into remaining quiet about what you want God to do for you. Give voice to those things! Go ahead and cry!

When you enter into real worship with God, He can minister to your needs; you can never get your needs met by losing your head. When you start murmuring and complaining, God can only focus on your unbelief. When you start resting in Him, He can focus on the areas of your life that need to be touched. When you calm down, God speaks. If you really want to be healed set free and restored, you must be in Him. As you rest in Him, every infirmity, every bent-out-of-shape place will be restored. Take the highway to heaven, and bring God into your life. This is the first step to becoming whole.

FACE THE DEMONS AND BE FREE

Have you ever asked your body, what happened to you? Haven't I always taken care of you? Maybe you need to have a serious talk with God about your body. With all the unhealthy things we engulf, our bodies are crying out for help. Let's be sensible, you are on God's time. Understand the theology of who God is. You have to live for God because testifying and being a firecracker for God is something that can't be reckoned with.

As you become more spiritual, you begin to recognize who you are, you distance yourself from those who are keeping you from God's promises. Then and only then will you find your purpose. God's agenda for you on this earth will end only when God calls you home.

Be excellent in the jobs God calls you to do. Be passionate in your walk with God. You see, God will push you into the place He wants you to go, God puts you in places and situations – you have no idea what's on His mind. God will prep you for His mission. Don't forsake your calling. Continue to think highly of yourself in spite of all earthly situations. God put victory in your path, you are a seed of greatness. Good and bad will be thrown at you, it's up to you to choose the road that will lead you to God's kingdom.

In the eighth grade, I was chosen to perform in a play called "KATS." Our costume was black leotards with black tights and a long black tail. Our faces were painted to resemble a cat. That play was the highlight of something huge in my life. That was the beginning of me being exposed to an audience.

As I look back, I can see God pushing me in the direction He wanted for me. Pushing back the darkness in my life, persevering was my outlet to be the person God wanted me to be.

I know for sure you can run all you want, but until you face the demons that have your mind, you will never ever be free. I carried demons for a while thinking everything bad that happened to me was my fault. But I came to grips with myself and I stopped the madness that had me bound and thinking I was a bad person. There is no greater joy than to allow God to set your mind free. God is our refuge and strength. We can lean on Him. We can talk to Him. God will not judge us

– whether we are weak or strong He will always come to our aid. God has given me the strength to fight off all demonic spirits. I keep my faith and let no one tarnish my thoughts about my God. I know I am blessed and highly favored. I will serve God until the end of time. People, I belong to the Almighty. My heart and soul are in His unchanging hands. When that day comes when He calls me home, I will know it is finished.

LAY ASIDE YOUR GARMENTS

In 2012, I visited Jerusalem. While there, I visited the Upper Room. If I recall correctly, Mahalia Jackson sang a song entitled *In the Upper Room*. The Upper Room was a small, but fascinating place. It was there that the disciples witnessed their Master stepping down to become one of them. He laid aside His garments – not only for those twelve men but for us all. He came to earth stripped of the glory He had enjoyed with the Father before the foundation of the world.

This was no time for form or fashion. Real ministry is done with a complete loss of distinction. If Jesus was to leave a lasting impact on those men in the Upper Room – that little ragged band of disciples, He had to cover Himself in humility. The final touch of God was delivered through a man who humbled Himself. He was dressed like a servant, ready to help the hurting. His ministry was best seen when wrapped in a towel.

If you believe God would exalt you, if you believe you have the ability to wash the dusty sand of life from the feet of this world, then please don't join the spiritual elitists who are impressed with their own speeches. Lay aside your garments – every distraction, every distinction, and put on the warm towel of servanthood. Lay aside your garments and serve. If you are only concerned with what you look like, you are going to be a very shallow, superficial person. People are going to find that once they have quit playing with you, the box you came in was beautifully wrapped – but empty. Go back to the source of your attractiveness, the Holy Spirit of God. When you are His, He will draw you to the right people for the right purposes at just the right time.

Do you realize when you love yourself, it will be so easy to love others? God has put in you the instrument to love and understand the meaning of loving the Master (God). He does not want you to worry about anything, He has shown you that He clothes the lilies of the valley and enabled you to get where you are. You of little faith, search your soul and realize God is on your side. He will not let you down. Sow the seed, and live the life God has for you. God finished it, now you have to carry it and make it a part of your life. Don't let a dime or dollar come between you and God. He can make you or break you.

Make every day of your life count for something. If you are faithful over a few things, God will break out a harvest for you that no man can stop. Bitterness does not function in creativity. How you think is the measurement of how you live. Push for greater things. The purpose is to walk in your destiny.

SPEAK FAITH

We should realize we are ambassadors for God. We will make mistakes. God will not hold that against us if we act like people of God. You are bound to rub off on someone. Have a good relationship with yourself. Don't sell yourself short by trying to be like someone else. It's tiresome and demeaning to God and yourself. I call it the messiness of life. Take the high road, God has the upper hand. Take that chip off your shoulder. Today is a gift, once it's over you cannot get it back. The pain of letting it go is less than holding on to it. If we will live the way Jesus wants us to and don't get bitter when things don't go our way, Jesus will give us a standing ovation. Those lingering problems can keep us from our destiny. Speak faith over your situation and become healthy and whole. Get rid of the same old song. God knows you have issues, let Him fix them. If you are a servant of the Most High, He will bring you out of your misery.

Have you ever been locked in fear? It's a debilitating ordeal. Sometimes, your situation can look so horrific that it creates fear. Circumstances should never push you to commit suicide. The enemy will stack the deck against you, but if you have faith in your walk with God, He will be yours consistently. The devil cannot come at you on a first-grade level – he will have to try a new way to attack you. Wait on the Lord, He has your back. God has the power to fight the enemy. If God gives you power, no one can take it, but if the devil gives you power, anyone can take it. God can show you the error of your ways, knowing God can put you in a compromising state where you will be His in every way possible. God is the most mind-blowing spirit. God has the most powerful, amazing, and caring spirit to ever touch the souls of men. If your situation seems to be troublesome, God is the hope of a new beginning.

NO ROOM FOR SELF-PITY

Don't put on a self-pity act to get people to feel sorry for you. Those people are not helping you. They are feeding your problem, throwing you under the bus, pushing you further into depression – that's not the way to go. Drive the bus, pull yourself up and begin to search your soul; you were not meant to be under anyone's feet. Escape those unresolved issues and live because the joy of the Lord is our strength. God did not promise us easy days.

If we get out of God's way, our blessings will find us without a struggle. God is in pursuit trying to chase us down with an abundance of blessings. Stand still and wait for Him. Set your mind free. Choose to live an amazing life for the will of God. Jesus is full of grace, goodness, and truth. Even if you are in a terrible situation you are not alone. Don't feel sorry for yourself. Pursue happiness. God sees you. That reminds me of the man lying by the pool complaining that no one would help him get into the pool. God said to him "get up" put on the whole armor of God and receive your glory. You have to live beyond your feelings. Get upon the right hand of God. Set yourself free from negativity. Point your thoughts in the right direction. Your excuses are just a wrong turn. Stop comparing and step up your game to be the person God anointed you to be. Before you see yourself moving forward, you have to get rid of the "poor me" excuses. You are not limited; God knows all your gifts. Start developing the greatness in you. Stay open to new ideas, open your mind, and exercise the right to be a child of the highest God. Excuses are nothing but a crutch. If you stay in faith, God will take your wrong and turn it into something great. You may have had some bad breaks, but there is no point in looking back. Full speed ahead. Good times are on the way. Put your faith in line with God's promises. Your rough start can only result in an outstanding finish.

God will always be faithful to man, but man will not always be faithful to God. Your sins will not stop salvation from working in your life. When you are not faithful to Jesus, your chances of prospering become limited. Jesus being on the cross has proven that His work is done. Stay empowered, your work has just begun. Now, you must line your faith, word, and works with God's promises.

When people throw dirt on you, just throw it behind you. The enemy wants you to become discouraged, don't lay down in misery, pick up your cross and keep walking holding on to God's unchanging hand. God will take you to the next dimension. Give God the glory, and He will give you peace.

You cannot sin your salvation away, you can only renounce it. If you keep sinning, it will harden your heart, whatever is not done in faith is a sin. Sinful actions will not cause you to lose your salvation; when you have a taste of the Lord, it is hard to forget Him. How can you reject Him when He has kept you from all harm and danger seen and unseen? You were not born in this world because you were a sinner. You were born in this world because of sin. All of this disobedience started with Adam and Eve. You know the story!! Seek God first. As soon as you wake up in the morning start praising God. God can bless you in the middle of a drought. Miracles are made out of need. Poverty is a mindset, you have to break it. God will test you in every way.

It is possible to live without Him, but is it safe? Will you live a good and prosperous life? Based on my life – I will not take a chance on doing anything without God's approval. No matter what it takes, you must use each day to worship and praise God for the strength and will to make each hour and minute count. God wants to meet your every need. Keep asking, keep knocking and everything that God promised will come to pass. It just goes to say, when you are at your best for God, He will do His best for you. Satisfying God is not hard. What is impossible to man is possible for God. You have only one life to live, fill it with things you wish to do. You cannot live a powerful life having pity parties.

■   ■   ■

Chapter **10**

In the Midst of the Storm

In my younger life, I've watched families torn apart by incest. There was a family that lived across the street from my family. The wife came running out of her house saying "Lord have mercy." I was about ten or eleven. I really didn't understand what the situation was about. Later I found out her husband and her daughter were having sex. The daughter was twelve. Later she became pregnant by her father. During the late fifties, you didn't tell people or the police. You resolved the situation among family.

I wonder what was on the husband's mind and the daughter's mind. I cannot determine if it was a warning for the wife or if the devil was determined to break the child or wife's spirit. Where is the love in this situation? All it takes is one person to tear a family apart. We all need to know the power of vision. Keep our mind on the positives, not the negatives. Let us pray for our children.

When you walk through a storm, you must lift your head up high. Put your shoulders back and walk with the intelligence God gave you. God said if you lean on Him, He will catch you. God will give you the joy He promised. Do not be afraid, you are not alone. He's not there just to hold your hand. You have the most confident and the boldest spirit with you. Some of us step into situations we cannot handle. Every now and then you will need your confidence lifted. God will strengthen you and give you the blessings to accomplish the things you cannot handle. Most of your life, you have seen God reach down and pull you out of situations. He will step in when it looks like it's over. No matter what; keep walking because God will do the pushing, He will do the supernatural. Our job is to bring people closer to God, not judge them. We are ambassadors of the Most High, we represent Jesus. God wants us to believe and trust Him. We have struggled to long and come too far to take steps backward. Don't give up on righteousness. Stay focused! People go through their own personal hell trying to find the righteousness of God who has never left them. God will always have a plan for you. Go to God – peace and joy are waiting there for you. Allow Him to crown you and celebrate you. You are His most prized possession.

God can work with anyone. He can cleanse your spirit and correct your behavior.

- Worship – praise God
- Prayer – change will come
- Recognition – Knowing God
- Repentance – change must happen

BROKEN TO BE STIRRED UP

Sin is such a factor in our lives. Miracles will happen only when we go to God in prayer. When we are in great need we must run to Him to conquer our most disturbing problems – sometimes, God has to wash you before He can bless you.

All your doubts and hopelessness have to be cleansed and removed in order to hear what God is saying. During your life, you have been rejected, and you feel emotionally drained. All your goals and dreams have been destroyed. It's like being in a swamp with no hope surrounding you. "What do you do?" Look to the highest mountain, God is within reach. He knows you are lost. If your burdens are still hanging on and you don't know how to release them, you must worship in spirit and truth. When you feel the acceptance of God, there is no turning back to the way you were. Old habits in your old self dissipate. You are a new person. God wants to see you – the person He worked so hard to create prosper and become His most valuable follower. You can do this. There is nothing hard about following God, it's always a pleasure.

You cannot live in this world without the love of God and expect peace. Thank you God for uncovering my eyes so I may see all the good you have done in my life. Everybody needs somebody in their life to push and love them. You can be smart, but not smart enough to do it by yourself. You will need a divine breakthrough. Your pain and disappointments only mean He is breaking you to stir you up, get the best out of you and elevate you. Surround yourself with strength and integrity. You don't need anyone but God to tell you about your needs. Your weaknesses and temptations will remind you of how much you need God. God will show you signs to give you strength to reach your potential. If God is not removing your thorns just keep honoring Him. You can be promoted with preparation. If you don't have the character to handle it, you will waste your time. Your character is more important than your talent. Can God trust you? Stay in faith. Secrets create frustrations. Continue to be yourself, God is changing you, He's testing you. Everyone is dealing with something. Don't let it sour your life. Be at peace with who you are.

BOLD AND OBEDIENT

Have you ever gone through periods of crying for so long, you water your own seed? If you fight your way up, then you owe no one anything. You only owe the Lord. The more you give the Lord, the more He gives back to you. The more you praise Him, the more He blesses you. Don't let the condition of your life destroy your dreams. Ask God to remove thorns from your life and believe God's grace is sufficient. Faith is trusting God when life doesn't make sense. If you're going to reach your highest potential, dig your heels in and fight the great fight. Many times, people have talked you out of your next level and fear when there was nothing to fear. If you are going to fear someone, fear God. Nothing can stop fear but the love of God. When God gives what He gives He will protect. When you pray, write the devil off. Don't feel convicted, acting on your feelings is not the way. Believe in the Word, you have the power. Free yourself from bondage and self-pity. Stay away from judgmental people. You can live courageously. The more time you spend in prayer, the more stress-free your life will be. Be determined and relentless. Go to God boldly and ready to be obedient.

We can't accomplish anything without God being at the head of the table. Always remember, being on God's team is the most outstanding and royal pleasure that we can ever acknowledge. We should stand tall and appreciate the love God has given us. Our lives depend on God Almighty. There is no greater understanding than the true meaning of love, honor, and respect for God.

SHOW LOVE AND RESPECT

Respect the elders, help them in every way possible. After all, most of them paved the way for us. God has given us the ability to take care of others. We need to embrace one another and show love and peace. Have you hugged someone today or maybe said something nice to someone? People, lay down your pride! Reach out and lend a helping hand. Wake this world up and show what God has given us. Remember, what you have achieved is not yours to keep. You have to show God your appreciation by giving back. Speak peace into your fellow man's spirit. Let goodness and kindness pour out of our mouths, take a stand and save ourselves from destruction.

God puts us on this earth to teach our babies and children how to love and respect each other. God never wanted the killings and robberies the tears and tearing down of our communities. Our forefathers fought hard and took too much back lashing for our freedom, now we're acting like animals. Senseless!! Take hold of your life, let God see you are making some headway. God has given the tools you need to become successful, use it for His glory. Listen to the cry of our young ones. God will save those who are crying out. We as adults have to stand boldly for God and set our minds on getting ourselves and others right for Him. Who we worship here on earth will determine our eternal life. Continue to talk to our young people, prepare them for the coming of God. We have the power and authority to show our young people how to prepare to embrace the Word of God. The battle will be won!

TIME TO MULTIPLY

We can do whatever we want through the strength of God. It's amazing how much we depend on our feelings when we are young. As we become older, we begin to rely more and more on God's Word. Please don't let fear be the ruling factor in your life. We can do this, we are a part of a great group: Father, Son, and the Holy Spirit. Some of us have overcome drugs, abuse, hatred, ridicule, judgment, loneliness, and hurt just to name a few. Be bold about your faith. You may be afraid to go through many things, but going through whatever you went through only made you stronger. God has already worked it out for you. Whatever Satan did to you, God will equip you to conquer.

I believe if we continue to seek God, we will unequivocally accomplish our goals. Life is full of opportunities – embrace them. God has shown us so much goodness. God is relentless, He has comforted you, paved the way, opened doors and He never turns His back on you.

It's time to see what God sees. We have eternal forgiveness. Remember when you go through something and can't see your way, look to the hills because faith without works is dead. Look at faith this way. When you plant something and don't water it, it will die. You have to nurture it in order for it to procreate. Faith without works will not work. If you have been knocked down, don't stay there – take the high road and come back better than you were before. You are a precious seed even if you have to rock and cry yourself to sleep sometimes, your life has just begun.

When you understand the power of God, your troubles are always a target for the devil. You have to believe in yourself, you have to be doubtless. Challenge yourself to be the seed God planted. You have already been watered, now it's time to go and multiply.

■   ■   ■

Chapter 11

Live! Cherish! Embrace!

Is Jesus enough? Get the turmoil and injustice out of your life. God pruned you to get all the ungodliness out of your life. Have you sinned willingly? Of course! We all have. Repentance will remove sin if you are sincere. Do you know there is a penalty if you continue to do so? Do what's right, be better today as opposed to what you were the day before. Keep the Word of God first. Develop a plan of good behavior and attitude – let peace rule your heart. This is your season to hit the home runs. Be a batter on God's team.

Have you ever caught yourself between intellect and instinct? It will take hard work to become knowledgeable and to understand the process of instinct. God wants you to step into your dreams. Don't make the mistake of judging people for who and what they are. Don't drop your head at any cost, face your demons head on. You created your problems, it's you who have to get rid of them. Whether it be finances, people or obstacles, you will have to stand on the level you are bargaining for? God doesn't want you to buckle for anyone. You will answer to God.

There are those who will criticize you and the work you perform. Keep your faith, stay on the wagon of truth and continue to do God's work. Faith is the evidence of things we cannot see. If you have a big heart, you should be able to do big things in life. Build your dreams on solid rock. Go get your blessings!

ON STAGE WITH GOD

God has armed us with tools that can change the world. We have to encourage our young people to go forward and accomplish their dreams. They are our future. Take a moment and reconnect with God. Tame your tongue and be a blessing to everyone you come in contact with. God is in your show; turn on the lights you are on stage. Your performance for God will determine your destiny. You are a champion. Expect greatness, God has amazing gifts waiting for you to tap into. Take the ladder to the highest. Doors are there for you to walk through, open them and run to the favors that are waiting for you. Don't let mediocrity get inside of you, stay free of additions and small minded people. Learn to walk in your destiny. God is waiting for you to live the big life.

Stay in agreement with God. The doors are open for you. Your parents laid the foundation. Take it and run with it. Live the good life that is out there for you.

I have a friend who always seems to get things going in the direction she wants her life to go. It seems she can get to the peak; however every time, things seem to change for the worse. She started a daycare center that failed because I feel she trusted the people who she thought were her friends. She lost her license for that business. Later she started an adult day care – that started wavering. Unfortunately, it is very hard for her to hold on to her dreams. If you have a passion for anything, put God first, keep Him there no matter what. God will answer you and show you how to attain a promising business. God loves to see His children accomplish their goals. God puts dreams in us that we can handle. Depend on Him to see them through. Remember, you and God are the majority. It's now or never!

God has prepared you for a wide and spacious life. He gave you a mind to read and to make your life comfortable. God is your supporter. If God declares he has your back, it changes everything. God will handle your business. There are saints employed by God who walk around looking for people to bless. Be aware of the people you mistreat. God knows every move and ever word you might think or say. It's very scary to come against somebody who has a strong belief in God. Take my advice, learn more about how God can work in your life. The opportunity to know Him is the best move you will ever make.

God has a way of moving swiftly through and out of your life. Everybody is not happy with the way God handles things. But, the problem is, you cannot see what God can. He understands you are human and cannot see beyond the next minute. God will bless you, but be prepared to lose friends, when God moves you up, your friends move out. When that happens, fight them on your knees, not with your fist.

SHIFTING GEARS

We were not born to be failures. God will shift you into second gear to help you meet your potential.

When I got married, I had to shift gears. I changed to a full-time responsible person. I wanted possessiveness and structure. I became a role model for my children. My goal was to teach them the goodness of God. I knew the road it would take to show them how God worked. I was willing to put all I had into giving my very best.

In doing this, sometimes, I let my emotions get out of control. Emotions can take control a lot in your life, education, jobs, and families. If you don't let the Lord lift you up, you will never see that your situation is bigger than you. Don't remain average, accept your responsibility, your children are looking for your input. Give them the education and guidance they deserve. Don't use excuses to justify shifting blame. You are the parent, serve your children well. Show your children how to build each other up. If you have a family, treat all the kids with the same respect. Just remember, each of them is watching you. Mistakes will be made, correct them ASAP. There is no room for lingering in hate and discontentment. Work with each child giving each one time with you. No two children are alike; each deserves your attention. Be aware, they grow up so fast. Time waits for no one. Love your children with all your heart.

Now, it's time to turn your attention to your spouse. Tell your significant other how good they look. Praise your partner, be gracious. Give your partner breathing room. Trust and let them know you are in their corner no matter what. You also need a life of your own. Each of us needs a lesson in how to live on purpose for God. The Spirit of the Lord will lead you to do what's right. If you want the Holy Spirit to lead you, let Jesus come into the center of your relationship. Everything breaks down in your relationship when you don't follow the grace of God. God is well able to keep you from falling. Circumstances will call you out of your comfort zone. Instinct shows you what life is calling you to be. God will always take you from the lesser to the larger. Your skills will not be discovered if you continue to hide the talent God put in you. Fly with the best, that's what God wants you to do. Be adventurous – live, love, build, and enjoy the life you once dreamed about.

WHEN GOD IS FOR YOU...

Don't be discontented with where you are, being content does not mean you are unhappy. God has you where you are because He is pruning you into your season. God's favors are chasing you. Don't become stressed or uneasy, God is working for you. Doing it your way is not the answer. Train your mind to be content and wait on God's Word. God has a lot in store for you. Blossom where you are, God has you on His radar. God does not promote discontentment. Live to rejoice and be grateful. Learn to enjoy the simple things in life.

If someone puts you down, not to worry, God will pick you up and take you to a higher level. Let your enemies talk. God is always listening. The power of God is in your spirit. He decided to make His bed in your heart. If God is for you, who can be against you. Don't sit around feeling guilty, God knows how to handle sin. God knows how to change your life and move you to another level.

In high school, one of the subjects on the curriculum was sewing using a power machine. Each of us had to make three outfits and model them at a commencement in order to get a passing grade. As I look back now, God was preparing me for the days ahead. I learned patience, control, planning, and principles. I'm so grateful I listened to God's Word.

Through elementary, junior, and senior high school, I learned a lot from my teachers.

THIS TEACHER TOLD HER TRUTH

An eleven-year-old girl trusted one of her teachers enough to reveal her secret. The teacher noticed how quiet the little girl was. This young girl stayed after class to talk to her teacher. She proceeded to tell her about the sleeping arrangements at home. Her mother put her in the same bed with her two brothers. Her brothers would touch her in places that were uncomfortable. She would cry out to her mother to make them stop. But her mother would only say "Shut up and go to sleep." She said to herself, how can I sleep with hands all over me. She would cry silently and keep fighting and hitting the hands that kept her from sleeping. She said that went on for what seemed like an eternity. Finally, after she turned twelve, her mother put her on a hard uncomfortable couch but her brothers got to sleep in a bed. One brother tried to continue what he had started. That ended when she started fighting with a very loud voice awakening everyone in the house. The teachers were afraid to confront the parents or the authorities on issues such as fondling or sexual harassment. Parents, please tell your children never be afraid to tell you if anyone touches them inappropriately. Be prepared to fight for your children.

God has a way of bringing the wounded out of terrible situations. That young lady went on to become a model citizen. She has overcome all of her anxieties and dilemmas.

You are a take charge person and in control of your destiny. No more letting someone get to your spirit, damaging your morals and lowering your expectations. No more allowing being touched inappropriately. The scriptures say that we are of God and when we see Jesus, all fear vanishes. Just one look into the warm eyes of a loving Savior can disarm everything life uses to assault our peace.

GOD NEVER FORGETS

God never forgets a labor of love. God has not forgotten your ministry. You may have helped someone to rise up and they walked away and forgot to thank you for your sacrifice. But not God. He never forgets. Just when you need Him most, He will show up.

> Now it should come to pass. If you obey diligently the voice of the
> Lord your God. To observe carefully all His commandments which I
> command you, that the Lord your God will set you high above all notion
> of the earth, and all these blessings shall come upon you and overtake
> you because you obey the voice of the Lord your God.
>
> (Deuteronomy 28:2)

You don't come to repentance without something escorting you there.

In high school, I became friends with Betty Boyd one of my classmates. We were such good friends; we wore each other's clothes. Betty was such a happy go lucky kind of person. God always put people in your life to give you a little more confidence, something I was a little short of. I realize confidence and self-satisfaction go a mighty long way. After over forty years, Betty Boyd and I are still friends. We both are grandparents and serving God.

We don't realize we are greater than our past. You are stronger than any moment of failure. No matter how foreign this place in your life may seem, you must know God prepared you for it. God shielded you and you are His. Safe and secure, you rest in the sanctity and safety of arms that will not fail you. The morning is yours. Spend it well. Use it sparingly. It is a gift. Nights will pass, tears will dry, and enemies will leave. But you will arise in the morning.

Some women have never been secure in the love of their natural father, and it affects how they view their heavenly Father. But listen to me, there is no doubt about His love. He made the ultimate sacrifice just to prove the authenticity of His love for you. Use your trouble to fill your passion. The depth of the trouble you have been experiencing probably equals the depth of the desires that drive you towards God. Don't allow yourself to be intimidated into remaining quiet about what you want God to do for you. No one teaches you how to transition from single to being married or from one job to another or from poverty to riches or from being abused to being free. You have to be the lion in your transitioning.

HUGS AND KISSES

Growing up, I felt left out, not needed or wanted. My parents were not the type to show affection. I was very shy and wanted so much to be liked. Every time I tried to be friendly I would get my feelings hurt. Very early in life, I decided to become a loner. I started focusing on my appearances and walking in my own truth. I created a lot of haters and speculations among my peers. That didn't bother me because I was getting a lot of attention. If you don't fall for the game, everybody wants to be on your team. They wanted to know what made me tick, or how they could become a part of team Joanne. Nothing bothers me more than being judged by people who don't even know your name. How can you call yourself a born again Christian when you can't open your mouth to say something positive about your fellow man, but you are quick to say unpleasant things and make inaccurate statements. LET'S GET REAL!

In this day and age, there are relatives who don't speak to each other. I'm talking about mothers, daughters, and sons. These are people who should be as close as possible. What backward person doesn't speak to their parents? Those people have no clue how God is portraying their actions. Listen – you only get one mother and father. What in the world got you so angry that you lost contact with your parents who stood by you, wiped your behind, cared for you, stood by your sick bed, clothed you, put up with your incompetence, guided you, spent money on you – I don't think I need to go on. But wait: When God calls your parents home, you are the very ones hollering and saying I didn't mean it. It's too late!! Don't you know we are not here to stay? Hug one another, love and be loved, you only have one life, live it to the fullest. Are you in harmony with God?

■   ■   ■

Chapter 12

Keep Walking

Sometimes, people you think are not good at anything know their purpose. Satan can imitate, but he cannot create. Start thanking God for putting those people in your life who mean you no good. They are the very ones who pushed you into your destiny. They made you stronger. Stop complaining about where you are. Sometimes, God won't give you what you want when you want it because he wants to give you time to get yourself together to be able to accept what He has for you. Thank God for grace. Satan is a divider. God is a multiplier. Satan knows the power of unity. You want to be at peace with yourself. In harmony, you can be in your range as long as you are on one accord with God. What do you know that heaven is unaware of? Don't be out of tune with God! When you fall, God does not turn away from you, He comes running toward you. Seek unity and peace, keep strife out of your life.

When you pray for someone, don't expect them to change immediately. God has a method for how and when a person will come into grace. Believe God for the grace He put in your life. The grace of God will have you doing much more for God and for others. Get way down deep in the innermost part of your heart, a flickering flame defied the blowing wind of disease and refused to be extinguished. A passion to live refused to die. OH, yes, I was sick and broken and lonely, but I was a long way from dead. I knew it wasn't over. My body didn't know it. My finances didn't show it. My family was gone, but I knew down in the chambers of my being, down in the basement of my feminine spirit whispered a hope that none could hear. The waiting game was over. I was a woman who was taking charge of my life. Now perhaps, you've been around the blocks a few times, made some mistakes and blew some chances and the enemy has said to you that you are beyond repair. But God keeps calling you by your name and not your shame. Listen to Him. You must hear God call you by name until you are so filled with whose you are that you forget what you have done.

GOD CAN STILL USE YOU

You are never too old for God. You are never too used up to be of service in His kingdom. A life's worth of lessons is yours. You have learned faith and practiced patience. You know how to listen, you have developed a friendship with God that can only exist because you have walked with Him day after day, year after year. You have stored the treasures of mercy and compassion in your heart, and you possess the secrets of seasoned wisdom that only comes with time. The Bible tells us that women are more precious than any jewel. As a jeweler admires and examines every facet of a diamond, the Lord looks at His daughters with the same sense of awe. Women are worth more to God than treasure. We as women are priceless to a man for many reasons. A woman's value is beyond appraisal. A woman accepts the realities of her life and works hard. We are cooks, managers, real estate buyers, investors; we make sure our families are always up to par when they leave the comfort of home.

I want people to look at me and see great mercies. I have a covenant of peace. My worship is the highest level of faith. You are not eligible to lead until you are eligible to duck all the knives and daggers that are thrown at you. The people who don't like you learn to pass the test. Don't let your situation intimidate you. Shut your mouth and let God direct your path. Use your intelligence, it will let you know when not to act like a fool. True leadership kicks in when you have to make a quick decision. Do you sometimes find yourself fighting battles that are not yours? God did not call you to fix people's battles. Don't lose your energy on people who have nothing to do with your destiny. You have to attribute your success to God's provision. When God tells you to be still, know that God is about to do something. Don't go by what you hear; go by what you see. God said that if I lose it in heaven, I will lose it on earth.

WALK IN THE WILL OF GOD

It's a new life, new day, new dawn. Let's rock with the Word of God. Never think you are too cute or too educated to be in love with God. If you think of yourself as higher than God, you will certainly wake up in the pit of hell. God doesn't play that. Put on your big girl panties and walk in His will. Lose that attitude, stay humble, pray without ceasing. Ask for more of God – you know you can't make it without Him. You've walked on the wild side long enough. God doesn't deal in auditions and callbacks for His children. He has something for you that only you can do. You don't need to be jealous or be intimidated by anyone because when God calls you, you are the only one who can answer. Life is about facing reality and being victorious over all obstacles.

Many years ago, my mother taught me a song called "Old Rugged Cross." I was fourteen and I sang that song in church. That song resonates with me even today. I sing that song quite often and when I do, it takes me back to the very day I performed it. I thank God for keeping me in touch with reality and keeping me grounded. The fine memories God has blessed me with will never go unappreciated. I serve a God who will move me in such a direction that I can carry on and on until the day is done. Be patient, wait on Him because He is worthy. God knows when it's your time to prosper. God has tied and bound you up to protect you from yourself. Fight your battles in Jesus' name.

Do you know the power of a shut door? When God shuts a door, there is no purpose in trying to pray open, work open, or pry open it. That doesn't mean the door cannot be opened. It just means that no human can open it. By now, you should know that He does what is best for you. There is a difference between a door Satan has jammed and a door God has locked. I can understand why hearts sing when the hand of God moves the obstacles out of the way. The eye can see the way made and the feet begin to dance toward a brighter future.

HE HOLDS TOMORROW

We live each day not knowing what the next day will bring. You will not always be able to see what tomorrow holds, but it is a great comfort to know that your God holds all your tomorrows. Tomorrows are not in the hand of your boss, your children, your husband or anyone else. It is not yours to manipulate or to dominate. Tomorrow is in the hands of the Lord. God will be there when everyone has turned their backs on you.

No matter how dark the night, you've always lived to see the light. Understand that God's grace has protected you, provided for you, brought you through, secured you and comforted you. His comfort is sure for every tomorrow.

It is so sad today that many girls will never experience first-hand the love of an earthly father. Somehow, they have been denied the privilege of cultivating a wholesome relationship with their natural father. However, they will recapture what they lost as they come to know their heavenly Father. It is wonderful to realize that the Father stands ready to reveal His love in your life. If you are such a person, the time has come for you to come out of it, allow yourself to feel again, allow yourself to cry again. Allow yourself to call out to God again. It's time – if you are willing, the Holy spirit will over-shadow you and the hidden Christ who has been locked up behind your problems, your fears, and your insecurities will come forth. You will see the power of Jesus do mighty things in your life.

> Whoever desires to come after me, let him deny himself, and take up his cross and follow me. (Mark 8-34)

My people, it is time to let Jesus take control. He is much better resolving our problems than we could ever imagine.

When sin abounds, God can take a bad situation down a path to a good situation. Choose a path of forgiveness, end your struggles, give them to God. Let prayer and meditation lead you on a profound journey. Trust God, you have not been

overlooked, you are being reserved. Your isolation is on res-
ervation for when the time is right, that's when God will call
you. You're just one step away from your purpose. You are
under God's agenda, what used to own you, doesn't work anymore. God has demanded your release, no more drama – you
are free!

YOUR FUTURE IS SECURE

As a small child in South Carolina, I would wake up early just
to hear the rooster crow. To me, that was the most beautiful
sound I have ever heard. I listened to my mother rattling pots
and pans preparing bacon, eggs, and her floating biscuits.
My God – my mother could cook. Her biscuits were so light
in weight so delicious and mouthwatering. I remember her
chasing chickens to prepare for Sunday dinner. She used a
big black pot with boiling water to put the chicken in, which
made it easy to remove the feathers. I watched her wring the
chicken's neck, all I could think about was – I just finished
playing with that chicken. As a child, I always wondered if this
was what God wanted for that poor little chicken. I couldn't
imagine God wanting to let anything die. I couldn't understand why people or animals had to leave this earth. But in
God's own time, He taught me the gifts of all creatures. As
we grow into our own, we learn about certain things we did
not understand as children. God always prepares us for the
unknown or for what will benefit us in the future. Learning
gives us survival skills, use them because life will throw you
some curves that will make your head spin. Embrace your
accomplishments, raise the bar higher.

You will run across resentful people. Hold on to your goals.
Put all your cares in God's hand. Don't beat yourself up, keep

the faith, God is a God of many gifts. Come into His peace and rest there. Don't be dominated and controlled by everyday problems. You have a serious relationship with God that exceeds all. You are a vessel for God. Your love for God will conquer all. As we grow older, it becomes harder to accept people who are against God's will. We will defeat ourselves because we are not united with the Word of God. I've been hurt enough to know how to be affected to please God and not others. Simple, you should not care about being liked. If you've been beaten down, scorned, abused, and not appreciated, understand this – the love of God will conquer all. There are devils who will try to take your mind, but the Devil should have read his Bible because you belong to God, the protector of your soul.

STOP, SMILE, AND SMELL THE FLOWERS

God did not hang on the cross by mistake. There were manipulations, lies, and envy. People get nervous when they see you gaining an audience, being recognized and moving up. People will plot against you because you got a little too bright and interesting. The Devil in them tries to damage your image. Watch out for those who are always in your face looking, lurking and asking questions. Keep walking and standing on the faithfulness of God. Even when your heart has been broken, and you don't know how to go on. Don't commit to being under attack, don't let the devil shut you down. Keep the Word of God in first place. God is standing by with open arms. You are a testimony that God is real. Try not to get in God's way, He wants to fix things for you. God has made provisions for you, work with Him, not against Him. Make yourself available to be a blessing to others. Sometimes, I look back and ask myself how I got over. I know serving God is the only way to gain His attention. I am guided by His powerful hand; there is not a shadow of a doubt that if I had not been obedient to God, I would have been dead in my grave. God saw it fit to give me a first, second, third, fourth and fifth chance to get it right. Learn to enjoy the life you have been given, no matter how insignificant it is. Ask yourself how much of your life you enjoy. Stop, smile, smell the flowers and enjoy your surroundings. Stop building mountains of troubles and struggles, it's not about what we are doing, it's about our attitude; set your mind on all the opportunities God has given you. Check your itinerary and act on it. Don't become passive, expect something extraordinary to happen. Live with the greatest expectations. Know the truth about God's love. He wants to be involved in your everyday life.

Know this – the church is not a perfect place. It's a place to be transformed. Delight yourself in the Lord, and He will give you joy and peace. You are God's daily delight. In the middle of trouble can you have a delight in God! When it's difficult, He will change your desires to match His. Know this – your success is in Christ. You cannot deal with the Word if you cannot understand it. God is on the loose, He can pull you out of night clubs, wipe out your sins, and make you operate on a different dimension. It's strange how life will take you around the same circle and land you on a much greater and more plentiful level. That's God working it out.

LEAD THE WAY

Set your sight on things above. Don't hold yourself back, be prosperous, lead the way for others to follow. You have been given the torch, run with it. Your way has been made plentiful by none other than the Almighty the Great Thou Are.

I ask God to bless my house. I know He can do it because I have seen Him do it for others. God has never lost a battle. I remember my brother was in the hospital, he was very ill. My sister called me at work asking me to come because she was told to gather his siblings. I prayed all the way to the hospital for God to let him live until I got there. When I arrived he had passed. But I also remember before I got the call, I was sitting at my desk seven thirty in the morning; I felt someone standing behind me, for some reason, I couldn't look back. I knew it was my brother, it was about the same time he had passed, and he came to say good-bye. James let me know he had moved on.

Even today, I can remember the very feeling I encountered in that eerie moment. God has a way of letting you know what He wants you to. Don't underestimate His gifts. Take them and use them to live a life of appreciation because you were given gifts for a reason.

The cross God asks us to carry is not for selfishness or to be self-centered. We have the life of God inside of us. Whatever your choice is in life, you will pay a price for it. If we chose the kingdom, we choose a great life. As we look around the world today, we know it's not working the way God intended. People who live with their heads held high acknowledging no one are headed in the wrong direction. Which road will you take? God's road or the world's road? This world is not your home. There is a high cost for low living. The choice is yours.

Ask God to touch you, He is pure, He will be waiting at the finish line. Just stretch out your hand. There is no other who can carry you the way God can. He can give you inspiration without interruption. Your faith will be tested, but never lose sight of God's goodness. He is my Rock, my Savior and my highest mountain, God is my all.

When Jesus talks, you've got to walk. God will accept you, no matter how many times people reject you. When you can understand the Spirit of God, He can deliver you from all wrong if you stay in His presence.

I worked for Equitable Trust Bank in 1968. My supervisor was Caucasian. She did not hide the fact blacks were not her cup of tea. With a passion, she conveyed to me that if her son married a black woman, she would disown him. I was shocked that she was so elated, bold, and carefree with her words. She did not believe in God at all. Before I left the bank, her physical appearance began to change, she was bent over with a hump in her back, and she could only look you in the eye if she was sitting. After I left the bank, I was told she had passed. God has a way of lifting you up or bringing you down. You can only be held by grace. People, we have a lot of work to do! God is waiting for you to get on board, join the holy wagon and ride with Him. He is the only way.

■   ■   ■

Chapter 13

Leaving Your Past Behind

In 1986, my God and I had a conversation about traveling. I said to God: "I want to stand on the same ground Jesus walked on. To my surprise, I was able to travel overseas with my friend Arthur Barnes. We have traveled extensively to London, Paris, Rome, Tokyo, Hong Kong, Europe, Belgium, Milan, Brussels, Bethlehem, the Sea of Galilee, and Macau. Lo and behold, I got the chance to spend eight days in Jerusalem. We visited God's mountain, the Wailing Wall, and the Upper Room, Now the ultimate – I stood on the very ground Jesus walked on. I have traveled throughout the States most of my life; traveling is one of my passions. When you are on the Lord's side, there is nothing God wouldn't do for you. I'm so grateful God saw it fit to bless me and keep me in His good grace to make sure all my dreams come true. I serve an awesome God. I honor God first in all my giving and thinking. I am so overwhelmed with the way God has directed my life. It's a miracle that I'm here to tell my story. God has kept me under His wings. I know no other way but to serve Him.

Those of us who believe in God will always have God's ear. God will look at us as righteous, holy and His instruments.

Stand tall in your faith, lean on God, he will be your rock. I don't want to leave this earth knowing I haven't encouraged someone to give his/her life to God. Sometimes, you will cry your way through things you have no control over, but God still loves us in spite of our past. He loves you through your pain, good and bad. He will not erase the plans He has for your future. Remember, storms come and go, there is always sunshine in the midst of a cloudy day. God has already wrapped you in grace and mercy, hold on to His unchanging hands; He is with you every step of the way.

God has made us strong enough to bear most pain – whether it's a broken heart or physical pain, all pain hurts. If by chance you become submissive to anyone and forget you have a mind of your own, that's a big mistake.

LOVE YOURSELF

A great lesson to learn is – let no one control your mind, dictate or mistreat you in any way. You have to love you, unconditionally, positively, and unequivocally. I took the time to ask God to wash me so I could make time for myself or to love me. God did just that. Now, I feel whole again – that, my dear people is what every person who has been mistreated, tossed aside, and walked on needs to accept and correct in order to live a peaceful life. Broken women will invite broken men. You will never learn from one another if you attract the same person as you; you will have to attract the opposite of who you are. Sometimes when we hit rock-bottom, God is the rock. We have to understand, God will always have our best interest first and foremost. People, love yourself and stay true to God.

There are two kinds of sorrow, happy sorrow, and sad sorrow. You can be the leading person in your own surroundings.

Start a tradition in your family. Help someone to find their wings. Keep feeding your wings until you are ready to fly. When your child cries out, you know when it's a cry that tells you something is wrong. When somebody changes your child's life, there is a rupture that breaks out in your soul that tells you your child is in pain or trouble. I remember at the age of eight, my son was outside playing with the kid next door. I saw the little neighborhood bully push my son, I watched for a while to see what my son would do. As I looked on, my daughter appeared, she waited until the bully hit her brother. My daughter told her brother, "If you don't hit him back, I will hit you." I saw my son pick up a brick and chase the kid back around the corner. I never saw that kid in the neighborhood again. I don't condone fighting, but sometimes, you have to stand up for yourself whether it is verbally or just walking away? As we become older, we definitely try to avoid all confrontations, which will make our lives more bearable and free.

DROP THE BROKEN CHAINS

I'm determined to have a life without chains, I will not be bound by those chains that have no meaning. The Lord said He will break every chain. My Lord is amazing! I have realized those chains were to remind us who is in charge. When others say you are nothing, God shows up and shows out. Keep letting God whisper kind and gentle words to you. If God can't fix it, it's not worth fixing.

How many of us have attended church so filled with misery and pain, hoping just to hear a word to replace that pain? That's when you are in need of just a little more of God. However, so many of us stray away from Him not knowing the return is always forgiving. They that wait on the Lord shall renew their strength. Just hold on a little while longer, God is able, trust and believe in Him. He cares for you. He will come through in the midst of your waiting. God will open doors for you. Be determined to have a life without chains. God doesn't have to move mountains for you, but He will give you the strength to climb. The Bible says your determination will see you through when nothing or no one else will. Start thinking about others who have a greater need than you. Send a blessing to the forgotten or the elderly who live on your block. Say a prayer for the sick and shut-in. Visit the sick or call an elderly person in your family, speak peace over this nation. God is our great supplier. I lift my hands up to God, as long as I'm with Him, I know I will be alright. Stay encouraged you are not alone.

This is the day the Lord has made, rejoice and hold on. I can't sing about Him unless I really love Him. Clap your hands and stomp your feet. I have learned sharing and living God's way will give you strength to walk in prosperity and love. What do you do when you think God has forgotten you? It's not easy when God seems so far away. Dismiss those painful thoughts. Sometimes, those tears are uncontrollable but don't worry. God will not fail you. You just don't know when God will show up. Trust Him, the pain you are experiencing is just a milestone. God has got you!! Hold on to His Word. He said He will never leave you nor forsake you. I have seen God break yokes in my life, surely, He will do the same for you.

Satan doesn't want you to win. Don't let Satan creep into your mind. If you give God the glory and stand back, He will handle Satan His way. There is nothing you can do but keep the faith and serve the Almighty.

MA-MA

One night, I heard my mother crying. That was the saddest cry I've ever heard. The next morning, I asked her why she was crying. She said to me that sometimes, you have to cry, and sometimes, you have to laugh but through it all God will prevail. I guess, I was too young to understand the meaning of her statement. As I grew older, I began to think about all the sayings my mother used. I now understand the little talks we used to have. My mother instilled in me the highs and lows of life. Nothing goes well all the time. You have to be prepared to take the bitter with the sweet. I remember ma-ma in a special way. She loved to sing while cooking or cleaning. This was her favorite song:

The Old Rugged Cross
by George Bernnard (in the Public Domain)

On a hill far away stood an old rugged cross,
The emblem of suff'ring and shame;
And I love that old cross where the Dearest and Best
For a world of lost sinners was slain.

Refrain
So I'll cherish the old rugged cross,
Till my trophies at last I lay down;
I will cling to the old rugged cross,
And exchange it someday for a crown.

Oh, that old rugged cross, so despised by the world,
Has a wondrous attraction for me;
For the dear Lamb of God left His glory above
To bear it to dark Calvary.

In that old rugged cross, stained with blood so divine,
A wondrous beauty I see,

For 'twas on that old cross Jesus suffered and died,
To pardon and sanctify me.

To the old rugged cross I will ever be true;
Its shame and reproach gladly bear;
Then He'll call me someday to my home far away,
Where His glory forever I'll share.

The lessons my parents taught me are very valuable. I will carry them with me for the rest of my days. I am a product of a Christian woman.

MY FATHER

One Friday afternoon, my friends and I were sitting on our steps. We were around twelve or thirteen years-old. My father was a great dancer. He asked us if we wanted to learn the dance called "The Madison." Of course, we were anxious to learn.

Back in the day, it was a line dance. My father lined us up across the block. He started calling out the words. He said – 2 up, 2 back fall into cha-cha, turn to the left, twist turn and fall back into the Madison. Before my father realized, there were 30 kids in a line stretched across our street – 312 S Fremont Ave. I learned how to swing dance just by watching my daddy. I've created lots of steps to include in hand dancing. I taught my youngest brother my creations. We would go to parties just to show off our new steps. Those were the days of just pure clean fun.

A FEW MORE WORDS OF WISDOM TO PARENTS

Too bad we had to grow up and face life's responsibilities. I look at kids today with all their gadgets; they don't talk anymore, there's always something in the hand or in the ears. Where did we go wrong as parents? Did we fail our children in the worse way? No, I don't think so, we have some very intelligent and responsible children in our midst. The media always portray our kids in a negative light. When I see or hear of a child doing the extraordinary, I commend that child whether it is on Facebook or elsewhere? Children should always be congratulated for all the positive things they accomplish. When children fail, we as adults should build them up. Give then something they can look forward to. Even if it's just you being present or a positive role model. It does not matter if you are the bi legal parent. Give an encouraging word. Contribute a donation to their education. Our children need us.

■   ■   ■

Chapter 14

Seeking God and His Righteousness

G od is for the wicket, but He is open to righteous. We must be in harmony and in alignment with heaven. God will forgive your weaknesses. If only you believe and trust Him with your life.

Women and men, please stop chasing after ministers and preachers, they are not yours. Many of them are married and well established or in a committed relationship. For God's sake don't lust after what's not yours. Those people have wives and husbands, families. "STOP IT NOW!" God has someone for you, just wait on Him. Stop paving your way to HELL. Believe in yourself. True love will meet you in its own time. Stop worrying about your life. Don't you know you are the righteousness of God?

"Shut your mouth!" As long as you are all up in God's business, yours will never be completed. God knows exactly who and what is best for you. Take a step back and re-assess. Seek ye first the kingdom of God for He is peace, joy, and happiness. Challenge yourself to always stay in God's grace.

Don't be ashamed of your past. Accept and receive! Let God determine your fate; when you support people who are trying to do what God expects of them, God will give you favor. You have directed a soul to Him. When God says meet Him at the door, you know there is a blessing coming for you. Run – don't walk, because you don't want to delay God. The Holy Spirit will keep you, but the Almighty will bless you. All our best days are in front of us. Know your God and when He is calling you, there is no greater love than the love you receive from Him. The warm blood that runs in your veins is a gift from the Great Thou Are. Seek Him every second of your life. Get to know Him, He can make you or break you. Stay in tune with Him. He will take you to the highest mountain and make all your dreams come true. He is the Alpha and Omega. The King of all kings. Never again insult His great sacrifice by questioning His love. You may not see it or understand it, but believe it. He absolutely loves you. Not just when you are right. He loves when you are wrong. That is what gives you the power to right the wrong you've done.

ALWAYS WORSHIP HIM

God wants desperately to heal the aching hearts that have believed the lies of life, you are special, vibrant, and full of potential and possibilities. You are so valuable that Satan held you for ransom knowing that your Father in heaven is rich! He asked God, "What would you give to see this woman freed? My heavenly Father sent His Son armed with love and wrapped in flesh. He said, "This is how much I think she is worth." His arms outstretched, Jesus hung His head between His shoulders and died naked on the cross. You and I mean that much to Him. He is waiting for you in a secret place. He will not fail you. He knows you inside and out. He will love you when all others forsake you. Jesus said today, tomorrow, I will still be on the cross.

I know plenty of people tried to take me out, but I woke up this morning with my mind straight on Jesus. Sometimes, you might feel the earth move. It may seem like the world is coming to an end. But it's God rolling away your burdens. Be still and know that God is in the building.

Seek the Lord and you will find peace. If you never do anything else, keep worshiping Him. He will instill encouragement like no other, He will speak to your heart, He will convey a message just for you, and He will crown you with His mercy. God will loose the chains that bind you. Go get your blessings.

If God favors you, and you stay true to Him, no one can touch you. Your character may be touched, but trust me, when God appointed you as His own, no one can bring you down. Don't let the evils of others dampen your spirit. You know, God can take a little and turn it into a lot. Do the best you can, with what God has given you. There is more to come.

If you can, reach out to a wide world of people, come up with solutions to problems and give comfort. God does not look at what you have accomplished; He looks at your heart. Let us lift each other up and keep in mind your reason for worshiping our Lord and Savior. Because, if you take Jesus out of the picture, you will only have HELL!

IF YOU WANT IT, IT'S YOURS

No one can make you have a bad attitude. You get what you believe in. A hopeful person refuses to be doubtful. Your thoughts and hopes are yours. Don't depend on feelings. God will do for you, just get rid of the bad attitude. Remember God is still on the throne.

Now pull off those ragged house shoes and that gingham dress, take those curlers out of your hair. Take a long, hot, luxurious bath and put on some perfume. If you want it, you can have it. Your father in heaven left you loaded. God doesn't want you to live with depression, He wants you to come out of your feelings of failure and rejection. It's time to choose life. God said: "Have I not commanded you? Be strong and of good courage: do not be afraid, nor be dismayed, for the Lord your God is with you wherever you go" (Joshua 1:9). Take heed and be aware, God will not lead you astray, He will not let you fight this battle alone. God's love is for everybody. If God wants you in a certain place, no matter what you are going through, you will be there – its non-negotiable.

I've thought about heaven quite a lot. What will God say to me, or what will I say to Him? They say the streets are paved with gold. I imagine angels all around inviting me in, and God waiting to take my hand welcoming me to the kingdom. I know what I have to do to get to that glorious place. I've made up my mind years ago to be obedient to God's Word. It has not been easy, but I trusted God and all stumbling blocks, nay-sayers and back stabbers have been removed. When people think they have me pinned down, my God comes back with vengeance. You cannot disrespect or fight against any of God's anointed people. All saints respect God. If you want to see God, your job is to be obedient and serve Him, not your ego or others. I have learned many years ago, you cannot depend on things and people to get you where you want to be. I look forward to that day to hear God say welcome home. There is no greater joy than serving the Lord. Can I get a hand clap, foot stomping praise?

Oh, how I love Jesus. My soul loves Jesus. He comforts me and stands with me. Sometimes, I used to wonder if I could make it through the night. With all the issues I had, everything seemed so bleak and uncertain. But I didn't give up. I held on, knowing I will be alright. I was never alone. Storms came and left. Burdens dampened my spirit. I used to say to God, "Give me rest and give me more of you." I wanted peace, joy, and happiness. I could hear God's voice saying, "My child, rest, I'm here with you. Let me wipe away your tears, and make you my own. Let go of your problems, cast them into the sea of forgetfulness you are surrounded with my love. You shall grieve no more. Live the life I have paved for you and sin no more. You are free!"

Do you believe and trust in God, and really understand the bondage He pulled you out of? No doubt, that's the meaning of true dedication and love. What a wonderful God we serve.

Let God's Word lead your life. Do not sin against God. I think about all the suffering Jesus endured just for us. They made jokes, despised, rejected, ridiculed, and crucified Him. Jesus took a dying breath for you and me. He even asked the Father to forgive us because we know not what we do. I want to give more than I have and more than I am. I want to learn to give what I'd rather keep, not a sacrifice of law, but a sacrifice of love. Give me more love than I have, so that I can love you more. Give me greater gratitude that I might be more grateful than I am.

BEING LED BY THE HOLY SPIRIT

Don't ever think you are alone; God is always with you. There is no greater joy than knowing God is in your presence. Step into the Spirit of God.

I grew up in a house where my parents were farm workers with very little education – but with lots of love, warmth, and pride. They would plow and cultivate the owner's land for cotton and tobacco to grow. The owner of the land calculated all their earnings. Most of the time, my parents were cheated out of their funds. I remember we relocated twice because my father did not allow anyone to come short with his money. Each house seemed larger than the one before. At night, the house seemed to take on a life of its own. It was said that people had died in the house and their spirits were still moving about. One particular night, I guess I was about four, I saw a figure of a man riding a bike passing the bedroom window. From hearing my parent's speak about spirits, I knew it was not my imagination. Even today, God lets me know when there is death in my family. I would get very scared and cry for reasons I can't explain. What I do is to start calling family members and relatives checking to make sure everyone is alright. When my parents, sister, brothers, aunts and cousin passed, I knew beforehand God was going to call them. I did not know when or where or how. I always prayed to God to take that gift away from me. God gave the gift to me, and He will help me monitor it. There were three of us with that gift. My mom and my cousin passed in March 2015.

MY STORIES

I was a member of a church for fourteen years. One Sunday, I sat at the end of the pew not knowing it was an assigned seat. The people started arriving and as they came in to sit in the pew where I was seated, I got up to let them in. Lo and behold that's when the trouble started. The older woman sitting behind me was saying I was in their friend's seat and I needed to move. All kinds of things were said. I thought to myself, "Who are these people?" They started tapping me and making crazy statements.

The lady seated next to them told them that they were wrong and asked them to leave me alone. Those three ladies did not acknowledge her at all. I did not move, I kept praying asking God to forgive them. It was very uncomfortable sitting there, but I was determined not to give them the right away. The next Sunday, I sat further up front. But three months later, that lady who led the three came to me apologizing with a big smile on her face. She asked for my name and wanted to hold a conversation. I was polite and resourceful. I knew God was in the building. I saw her six months later, she was using a walker. She returned to church once more, and I did not see her again. Later, I heard she had passed.

Sometimes, God just gets tired of His people acting "greater than thou." We have to respect each other and give our all to help those who cannot help themselves. God is always watching and waiting to see how we are serving Him. What goes around, comes around – make no mistake about that. Stop making other's lives uncomfortable. Does getting a laugh off others make you feel important? If that's true then you need a reality check. God has no use for underachievers – you can take that to the bank. Be respectful, love one another, help someone, go the extra mile, you will never ever regret being the bigger person. It's one thing to be free indeed. Looking over your shoulders is a bad decision. Stay free in the midst of obeying God. You cannot gain wisdom without making mistakes. Don't escape one prison for another. Look before you leap. Take your life into your own hands. Let God declare your freedom. No matter what your circumstances may be, God will set you free! A little bit of faith will be your destiny.

In 1999, I started to search for a new home. To my surprise, it took me one year to find exactly what I wanted. There were complications unknowing to me. I only had one outstanding debt. The lender came up with so many excuses for not financing the loan. I asked God "Why am I having these problems?" The voice in my head kept saying pay off your car. I wrote the check and mailed it. The loan officer couldn't find any other reason not to approve the loan. The next week, I received a call congratulating me on acquiring my new house.

I know firsthand that God delays some things in order to make a smooth transition. God knows what's ahead.

■ ■ ■

Chapter 15
No Condemnation

He makes life easy. When God talks, please listen and do exactly what He tells you. There is no greater joy than fighting the enemy when God has your back. Stay connected to God, He will stay connected to you. Isn't it funny how you bring the attitude of others on yourself just by being a pain in someone's behind? You lost your sense of joy, which affects everyone in your home and elsewhere. When asked a question such as "What's on your mind?" You reply "nothing" – you've lost your sense of communication, you need joy where ever you are, whether it is at home, job, church or in your car.

Listen – when the Devil walks through your grass, pull your water hose and just wash the Devil back where he came from. Look deep within yourself and find the word God put in you. Yes, it's there because God put it in your spirit. Create a thirst for God – He will quench your thirst. Glory and mercy are at your door. Open the door and let mercy in. It's God who is knocking.

At the age of eleven, in elementary school. One of the girls in my class would call me names. She did this often. One day, when she did this, my teacher heard her. After class was dismissed, my teacher asked me to stay behind. She sat me down and said to me. Joanne, don't worry about what people call you, just know and remember as you go through life, people will be mean and some will be nice. She went on to tell me how she was called the same name when she was in school. I couldn't imagine anyone calling her names because she was so attractive. Looking at her gave me hope. She told me to hold my head up and don't let people rattle my mind. I took her advice and used it to my advantage – it worked. Even today, I remember those words of wisdom. I saw Sheila thirty years later. She was suffering from an illness that was taking over her body. I said a prayer for her and moved on.

When you allow God to get bigger in your life, your problem will get smaller. You will see your peace return, your joy and new friends will emerge. God called you His masterpiece, stop allowing people to sink into your mind. Don't listen to the voice of shame. Rise up, count yourself blessed. Let no one make you feel unworthy. God will roll away the doubt.

When people cast shame on you, just say to them, "shame off of me." Don't let the enemy make you a victim. Stay strong, trust God. Take the lead and be the jewel God wants you to be.

Are you like sheep who graze in one area and do not move on? This is why we need a Shepherd – our God. We depend on God for all our needs, we may not want to admit it or acknowledge it, but we need God. God wants us to explore and become fruitful.

POWER OF PRAISE

Don't break the rhythm of praise to the Lord for anybody. No matter what you hear was said about you, no matter how people may look at you, no matter what happens, keep your praise going. There is power in praise. This is the way it works – while you are praising the Lord, He is fighting your battles in heaven. He is dealing with the enemy of your soul. He is pulverizing the demonic powers that seek to oppress you, bind you and keep you from His blessings.

Have you ever praised God singing and rejoicing as you were driving your car and, suddenly, you felt as if you weren't alone? God's angels were there right by your side.

You may not have seen them, but they were there. The Bible says:

> The angels of the Lord encamps all around those who fear Him, and delivers them. (Psalm 34:7)

If you can praise Him for the doors that have not been open, if you can praise Him for the mountain you have not climbed. When He has opened up His heart and allowed you to do these things, then you should not whine or complain because God has put you on a road to success. God will take you from one dimension of grace to the next level. Trust God on every level of faith, God has blessings for you that you haven't seen. Stand up and take responsibility for your future. Don't live with uncertainty, restore your life's balance. Win the battle from worry to worship. Claim the victory over your life.

NO DEVIL CAN STOP YOU

The devil is not after you. The devil is after your territory because He is afraid of what you may become. He doesn't want you to be what you were created to be. The devil enjoys attacking you, telling you that you will never be anything. Sometimes, you might have so many demons against you and the enemy keeps marching against you to bring you down.

This is not about you, it's about all the people you influence, your degree, your belief in God. You've got to believe you are much more than the devil says you are. God will deliver you. The devil wants you to sit in the pew and be a spectator, but the moment you start raising your hand and worshiping God, you will anger the devil. Stay in the presence of God. When you begin to worship, worry has to flee. If you believe in God, He will give you whatever you need. Don't listen to your negative mind, you know the devil is trying to persuade you to disconnect from the Word of God. Tell the devil to take his best shot. You are a person who believes and trusts in God. Be bold with your faith in God. Get God excited about blessing you. God's Word will not change. You can take that to the bank.

You cannot take prayer and use it to work the flesh by praying a certain amount of times or a certain way. God knows what you are doing. You may be sincere to yourself, but are you being a true worshiper? Pray from the deepest part of your heart. Fight for the will of God because as long as the devil is alive, you will run into the battles of the mind. The devil will toy with you on every level of your thoughts. Be consistent with your prayers. Keep your mind on the will of God.

LIVE BY GOD'S STANDARDS

Do you try to figure out what God is thinking? If you are, stop because it's truly impossible. If God wants you to know something, He will let you know in more ways than you can imagine. Learn to accept things beyond your comprehension. You have what it takes. If you allow God to direct you, there is nothing you cannot do. Do you know how many people are living together and are not married? In my day, it was considered a sin. Don't get caught up in the ways of the world. Honor God, live by His standards and respect yourself. Take your time and use your head for the goodness of God. He wants you to live a good and serene life. Don't do what the Jones' are doing, make up your mind to live a promising life of faith. Set an example for the ones who are watching your behavior. Your children and others who think highly of you. Stay in the limelight of good morals and values. Live a life of expectancy, let God open doors and pave the way. Keep your heart and soul on God and what He is doing in your life. Take my advice, I have been there and have no intention of repeating that episode.

As I look back over my life remembering all the negatives I encountered as a child, I realize those were stepping stones leading me to my destiny. As I grew older, I began to rely more and more on God's Word. I learned how to protect myself from all ridicule and predators. My God stepped in and showed me what it means to be loved by Him. I held on to God for dear life. I became the person God wanted me to be. God told me to hand it over to Him, and He will make my life a bed of roses. He did just that. Here I stand today writing about the goodness of God and how He brought me out of all the misery. I am happy and well contented. All my joy and peace comes from my Lord and Savior. No one can top that. I am truly blessed.

People will try to harm you in any way they can. Do not retaliate, humble yourself, stand still, give it to God, He will fight your battles. Let the presence of God enter into your soul. He will make your enemies your footstool. Slow your roll and wait for the Almighty to rescue you. He may not come when you want Him, but He will be on time. Be patient, He's at the door, just let Him in and your battles will be over. Now stand back and watch Him take over. God's works are as smooth as silk. He works when we are asleep. That's when God's performances are at their best. Don't move, lift a finger or render a thought, because God's got this. Give your heart to God, He will become your every desire. Just trust Him.

GOD'S SUPERNATURAL POWER

There is a song titled "There's a Storm in This Old Building." As you approach life, uncertainties will play a big part of your future. Storms will come, but God has given you intelligence to recognize trouble. However, the lack of knowledge of God will not prepare you for the road that lies ahead. Just remember to keep grace in front of you. Worrying will not get you there but holding on to the promises of God will. Let go of your burdens and position yourself to accomplish your dreams. The supernatural power in your life will save you from dangers seen and unseen.

Isn't it strange when you ride by a house and it has great curb appeal, you just know the inside is fabulous? That may be true but the family that resides there tells a different story. The house could be filled with hate, family members against family members, husbands against wives. Never judge the book by its cover. Don't wish for something you have not examined. Create your own thoughts and dreams. That's what God put in your DNA, you are so different from the next person. It's OK to dream but don't let others cheat you out of your future plans. Don't be overwhelmed by what you see, there could be turmoil in the making. Can you trust God when He says NO?

When you become a new creation, God makes you pure but do you became blameless? If you want to know what your spirit is like let your body and mind line up with the Word. That is the mirror of your spirit, you are challenging your mind to change. You have to choose the new you in order to dominate the old you. God gave you gifts to serve Him. Your talents belong to God. Use your gifts wisely.

> For as we have many members in one body, and all members have not the same office: So we, being many, are one body in Christ, and every one members one of another. Having then gifts differing according to the grace that is given to us, whether prophecy, let us prophesy according to the proportion of faith. (Romans 12: 4-6)

Here, the apostle Paul talks about how we are under one God. We have many members in one body but all the members do not have the same functions. We don't have to be jealous of one another. We have been given the same amount of body parts. Use your knowledge in your ministry. Please understand, nothing fuels prayer like need.

Neither the tranquil mood of a calming organ nor a dimly lit room with hollowed walls can promote the power of pray like the aching of a heart that says, "I need thee every hour." The presence of need will produce the power of prayer. You can accomplish anything once you have been called to Jesus. Jesus was the only one who truly knew me. He unleashed the potential that had been bound up for years. He can do the same for you. I can accomplish anything because I have been called by Jesus. From that moment on, I became invincible. The enemy, however, would love to destroy me. He will try anything. He will use my own words against me but the Lord told me the truth about myself. He told me I was loosed and set free. He saw the truth in spite of what everyone else saw.

When you begin to see yourself as Jesus sees you, you will muster the courage to break away. He is your defense. He will defend you. Don't give power to those who are not with you. Because what you put focus on, you give power to. Focus on Christ in you. You can be fully mature in Christ. Focus on the Gospel of Christ. Empower yourself with the obedience of Christ. My people, Christ is in all of us, tap into His glory.

HIS GRACE IS SUFFICIENT

The gospel of grace has nothing to do with us. It has everything to do with Christ. Religion told you things you cannot do for yourself. Benjamin Franklin said God helps those who help themselves. God never said that. Listen closely, what does it mean to go to church? It means to have Christ live inside of you.

> I do not frustrate the grace of God: for if righteousness come by the law, then Christ is dead in vain. (Galatians 2:21)

When you are the righteousness of God you are redeemed. God is where you are. Allow Him to take over your life. Focusing on Him produces change. He will not force His love on you, you have to receive it by faith. If you are so inclined to live a good life, recognize what He has done for you.

> But we all, with open face beholding as in a glass the glory of the Lord, are changed into the same image from glory to glory, even as by the Spirit of the Lord. (2 Corinthians 3:18)

You will see the glory of the Lord in you. As you study the Word of the Lord. You will be transformed into forgiving those who wronged you. God breaks yokes and bondages, remember, we are made in His image. Some people will grudge you for what God has allowed you to accomplish and they perform unforgiving acts to make you feel inadequate. Stand your ground, you are who God says you are – strong, intelligent, resourceful, and highly favored. Keep your eyes and mind open to the will of God. Don't be bullied by anyone or anything. You belong to God, not to the satans of the world.

He is the one who paved and provided you with the good things in life. God designed you to walk in your authority. Learn to triumph over the enemy, you can't change what happened, but you can change how you feel about it. We know new levels bring new devils. Listen, my people – people will try to destroy you. Preachers, bishops rise above your opposition because it's just your projections that will make a difference. This is your opportunity to let the world hear what you have to say. This is what God appointed you to do, this is your mission, your life.

BE WISE AS A SERPENT

Let's go a little deeper: The more people who love you, the more others will hate you. Your success on any level will create hatred. Be determined to be the best, even if you risk losing friends. People will grin in your face making you think they are on your page, be aware that your success is on the line. Be aware of roadblocks. Give information only when it is necessary. Everything that happens in your life is your responsibility. There are oppositions surrounding every successful person. Negative forces will follow you, look closely at the ones who are around you. Be careful and choose friends wisely.

Let's focus on your victories. What have you accomplished that you are not giving yourself credit for? Think about all the godly things you have done. Motivating people to be positive, encouraging someone to be a better person, showing up as you have promised, respecting others – just to name a few. God is looking at your performance. Stand firmly in your place, God is working on your behalf. Celebrate and enjoy what's in front of you. Give yourself a break and don't burn out.

Your mind will tell you what God expects from you. Your prayers will no longer be, "God give me." They will be, "God, make me a better person so I can serve you." Learn to focus on the joy God placed in you and how far He has brought you. If you love God and treasure Him, your life should be a big party rejoicing and praising the Lord for changing you from the person you used to be.

There is a battle between you and the flesh. The flesh will never be satisfied as long as it does not get its way. Don't live trying to please your flesh. You want to go higher and higher. Your feelings will take you down the wrong road. The flesh will not let you get beyond your potential.

A mature person will think about what he is saying and doing. You know you should bite your tongue, sometimes, the flesh can get louder than you think. But you will pay the price for it. Do what's right, say no to the flesh. If you want to see God's great favors, learn to do His will. I remember eating shrimp salad and ice cream. My flesh never said you are going to get sick. Your feelings tell you not to eat that combination. The Spirit of the Lord is awesome. Say no to certain things. Never let your feelings overrule you, take your feelings off the throne. Stop feeding those emotions, anything you feed will grow. Seek self-control! Older folks will tell you – "You reap what you sow, don't let your flesh dictate to you." Know who you are and what your body and mind can handle, it's the key to heathier choices.

God's favor will take you where you cannot go on your own. Energize your relationship with God and let Him lead the way. Let God determine your everyday life.

You are not the source of prosperity in your life – God is. The highest form of giving is to trust God. Give your life to Him, and He will give you your desires.

We have so much work to do. My mission in life is to bring more souls to God. Stay with me people, this mission is not mine alone. God is getting ready to change some things around. Keep your hand in God's hand and see the changes that are coming your way. Stay connected with our Lord and Savior. Shake the devil off because God's got this.

■   ■   ■

Chapter 16

Moving Forward

D on't you get tired of lying in a bed of laziness, despon-dency, and dysfunctionality? Get away from people who aren't going anywhere. Surround yourself with people who are not limited in the same areas that you are. Stop groping after things that are not for you. Take a stand, and move toward your destiny. You will never win if you don't face the unknown. God did not have a convenient life, what makes you think you will? This is the time to be creative. Develop a strategy to move to the top of your game. Be tena-cious enough to take a stand.

In my lifetime, I have tolerated a lot of uncomfortable situa-tions from people whom I thought cared about me. A person said to me, "I love you, but I can't stand you." I asked him "why?" He revealed to me, "You are independent, self-reliant, and goal oriented, whatever you go after you seem to obtain it." I pondered that for a while, pushed it out of spirit and moved on. I was raised by a strong black woman. My mother taught me to believe and trust in God and always set the bar higher than your last task. Stand on God's Word and be true to yourself. The lesson I've learned from God is to let Him fight the battles of all non-believers. This is when life becomes bittersweet. People will try to destroy your dreams. If anyone wants to push you, push back with the Word of God.

Sometimes, in life, you have to remind yourself who you are – you are excellent in your career, favored of God, a hard worker, rising to new heights, prosperous, the head and not the tail, lender and not borrower, disciplined, an overcomer, you do what you need to do, self-controlled, make good decisions, child of the Most High, a quick learner, good person, full of God's wisdom, compassionate, able to fill my destiny, strong in the Lord, more than a conqueror, competent, anointed, creative, talented, confident, grateful and empowered. God takes pleasure in prospering you. God did not give me the spirit of fear, worry, envy, hatred, jealousy, selfishness, and I will not accept them. God has given me good health, a healthy mind, healthy limbs, a good spirit, and an excellent attitude. My God has made me a happy woman.

SAY "YES" TO GOD

Have respect for what is sacred. The art of surviving painful moments is living in the "yes zone." We need to respond to God with a yes when the doors are open, and when the doors are closed. Our prayer must be, "I trust your decision Lord, and I know that if this situation is good for me, you will allow it to continue. I also know that if the door is closed, it is all for my good. So I say yes to you as I go into the relationship of spirituality." I know it is very important to understand the sovereignty of God. There must be an awareness within your heart, a deep knowledge that God is in control and that He is able to reverse the adversity. When you come to believe in His sovereignty, you can overcome every human trial, knowing that each one is divinely permitted and supernaturally orchestrated. God arranges these trials in such a way that the things that could have paralyzed you will now motivate you. When you know who you are, you don't have to struggle to live up to what someone else thinks you're supposed to be.

God wants to free you from the cords of manipulation, cords of blackmail, cords of emotion and bondage. Cut the cords that tie you to the old mud holes of your life. As you cut the cords, get ready for a new enthusiasm, a new outpouring of faith, a new freshness of anointing. God will release you to live in freedom. Let the cool waters of His Word rinse the residue from your past. Spread before Him every issue; He can't cleanse what you will not expose. Bathe your mind in the streams of His mercy. This kind of bathing is as holy as a christening and as refreshing as a shower, it brings the renewal that can only occur in the heart of a person who has been through enough to open her heart, to board up her past and to stand in the rain of His grace.

You are unique – that's what makes you priceless. The Lord will never, ever replace you. He has millions more children, each one is wonderful but none is exactly like you! Never give up your uniqueness in order to be what you admire in someone else. Glean all you can from everyone, but duplicate none. You are too priceless as an original to be reduced to a cheap copy! Don't let anyone manipulate you into forsaking your own uniqueness. Those people weren't built for your life's destiny, and they can't play your role. Aren't you glad that God prepared you for life, instead of preparing life for you? Redefine your purpose, gather your assets, and keep on living and giving. No matter what age you are, you haven't seen it all. No one knows how God will end His book, but He does tend to save the best for last.

REMEMBER WHOSE YOU ARE

Have you ever gotten up in the morning with a powerful thought on your mind and before your feet hit the floor, you were bombarded with thoughts of why you should not take that thought to the next level? Don't back down from the great thoughts God put in your mind. Push through all that defeat. I dare you to go forward because whatever God has given you to do, it shall be done. Whatever God tells you to do, the world will try to make you take two steps backward. Challenge the world with what God put in you. When God promises you something, and you think it's taking longer than it should, you begin to let those thoughts drift into your mind that God is not working on your situation. But the truth of the matter is – you need patience because God will not leave you in the cold. He always shows up when you least expect. Stop worrying because that leads you into wrong thinking. Don't make yourself miserable in the process of waiting. It's useless to worry about something you cannot control. It drains you of your energy. Get your eyes on Jesus, He is the Author and the Finisher of your life. Consider Jesus more that you consider your problems. Laugh more, love more, and trust God with everything.

We serve a God who has supernatural powers. We are blessed with the grace of God. No man will stand alone as long as we keep our hands in God's hand. We will be blessed above and beyond any obstacle that comes at us.

If you have your father's favor, no one can stop your blessings. Don't waste your time and energy fighting the opposition. If

God is for you, who can be against you. Just remember who you belong to. Faith will be strengthened through conflict and struggles. Don't be intimidated. Go for it!

Single people, your life should not center on a man, or a woman, for that matter. By God's grace and power, you can still receive the inheritance. If you have been walking around with a drab spirit and a broken heart, I am talking to you. If you have been in a state of depression that is robbing you of these precious years when you should be thriving and pursuing your destiny, hear this word. Don't waste another day in regret, sleeping away God's mercy, losing your chance to achieve and receive. Get up and get busy!

LET GOD FILL THE VOIDS

One of the greatest things we are afforded as Christians is the opportunity to receive restoration in our areas of depletion. Thank God that we have a Lord who can be touched by the feelings of our infirmities. He is able to minister to the voids in us. This ministry brings us to wholeness. That wholeness, in turn, makes it possible to live as if the brokenness had never occurred. First, you need to isolate the problem from the gender. You need to understand that all people are not the same. Isolating the problem brings healing. When you isolate your problem, you put it in quarantine and forbid it from infecting all areas of your life. When you isolate it, you stop the enemy from using it to rob you of good moments in the present because of bad moments in the past. You must allow God's love to pierce through the pain. It must be His love first. You can trust Him. It is with Him that you can learn to unleash the love you have locked up. It's your decision.

Unless you are able to accept responsibility for your actions, you will be eaten up with unresolved guilt. It will rot inside you and erupt in your life in the form of jealousy, anger, hatred, and bitterness. Identify the people you are blaming and deal with them. Accept your share of the responsibility for what has gone wrong and ask God to forgive you.

If you will face up to your own sin and take hold of the hand of our forgiving God, you can overcome anything.

My people, set your cup down, take the blanket off your lap, and stand to your feet! Have you not known, have you not heard? For every person facing winter – that is new life in your old age! Your past can cause you to look at life in a way that is less than God's perspective. As a young girl, I was abused. I had to learn to defend myself by not trusting men. A definitive attitude can accompany you into adulthood. If you have successfully protected yourself in a certain way in the past, it is natural to continue that pattern throughout life.

SET YOUR MIND ON GOD

Many people live with co-dependent relationships. Perhaps you have become so accustomed to your problem that even when you have a chance to be delivered, you find it hard to let go. Problems can become like a security blanket. As the Bible says in 1Chronicles 29:18, you've got to fix your thoughts, your attitude, and your whole heart on the living God. You can't expect the whole human race to move over because you had a bad childhood. They won't do it, and you'll just end up depressed, frustrated, and confused. Spare yourself the suffering. God is not in the business of punishing you.

God poured out all His anguish on Jesus so that we may have an abundant and profitable life. Why would you continue to pray to God to do something He has already done? God will not answer a pray when you know what He has already told you to do. God gave you the power and confidence to get what you need. Let grace lead you. Revelation tells you it's already done. Christ will always be inside of you.

Let the Holy Spirit bring you closer to God. Become a 20/20 for God, demonstrate your faith by giving your life to Him. How you think about things is how you are going to react to them. Stay grounded in the will of God because He is well able to bring justice to all. Accept people for where they are, on the way to where they are going. We all want to give victory lessons. You can improve your own joy by listening to your own voice. Shut out all gossiping and acknowledge what comes around goes around. When you have peace in you, the storms will be lighter. Do the right thing when you are thinking the wrong thing. Let's make a decision to live for God and not for man. You will have a joyful and less painful life.

Jesus will tug at your heart; all He wants you to do is let Him in. He has so much He wants to tell you, so you can live the amazing life you always wanted.

Hear me when I declare to you that the Father loves His people. His heart cries through the prophet Jeremiah for the healing of His children. He is broken at the thought of their brokenness. He is longing to restore them and to provide for them. Whatever the need, He longs to see it met. He is Jehovah, He is the father of blessings, and He is a giving God. He will bless His sons who are created directly in His image and after His similitude. We are not weak in terms of being sub-standard, but weak in terms of being softer. Weaker doesn't mean lesser, just softer, more satin-like. Rejoice in the soft-ness of God's loving arms. The Lord is your strong man, your hero, your Father who loves to bless you, and He never goes to sleep.

BE A BILLBOARD FOR SUCCESS

You don't know what's in you until something hits you hard. Do we as humans know the value in us to be resilient? Are you comfortable making decisions? If not, we can be taught to make wise decisions by letting God show us how to stand and take charge of our lives. Don't grieve over things you cannot change. Think of life in this way, I would rather be a billboard for success, than an advocate for a coffin.

Do you realize that God is the God of the unexpected? He said you will face trials and tribulations, but He will always have your back as long as you believe in Him.

Do you make withdrawals from God when you don't see benefits? The day will come when you will see God's uncon-ditional love. There will be something in your life that will make you fall on your knees and pray the prayer of help and forgiveness. Life will hand you somethings you never expected. Learn to be flexible because God knows your every weakness. Don't allow danger to lower your expectations. Success is never an accident. Some of the greatest challenges to our faith are those moments when we must endure the cold blight of a disappointment. The greater the anticipation, the greater the disappointment when we fail to receive what we have anticipated.

THE CHILD IN ME

I thank God for understanding the child within me. He speaks to my blanket-clutching, thumb-sucking needs. In spite of my age, my income, my education, He knows the childhood issues of the maturing heart. This is the ministry that only our Father can give. Have you ever noticed that to those who brought you into the world, you will never grow up? They will completely disregard your gray hair, your crow's feet, and your blossoming waistline. No matter how many children call you "Mom," to your parents you are still just a child yourself. They seem to think you have stepped into a closet to try on grown-up clothes and are really just pretending. They must believe that somewhere beneath the lines on your face, there is still a child. No matter how spiritually mature you try to appear, lurking in the shadows is some childish desire you just prayed away last night – the lingering is evidence of some tiny temptations. Only the Father can see the very worst in us, yet, think the very best of us. It is the unfailing love of the Father whose children should have been old enough to receive inheritances without acting like children, without wandering off into failure and stumbling into sin.

GOD IS IN THE GOOD AND BAD TIMES

"God give me the grace to forgive the things that seem insensitive. Give me the strength and creativity, patience, and humility. Make my heart race with the passion and affection that once came so freely. Father, teach me how to be a good person. Most of all, Lord make me like you. Hover over me. Fashion me for you Lord. Breathe fresh life into me again. Allow me to laugh and play again. Thank you for knowing what to do with my heart. I believe there will be a change because of you. I have cast my burdens on the Lord, and He has sustained me. He will never permit the righteous to be moved."

We need love when we have been treated unjustly, mercy when we have been misled, and peace when we have been disturbed. Our Lord and Savior can provide us with all that we need. Come with me, let us go into our kneeling position and pray the prayer of salvation. God is waiting, let's not disappoint Him. Open your heart and let God lift you up into the great world of peace. When you walk in the will of God – He will supply your needs, you have the right to claim His promises. Your life is a treasure to God, stay in peace.

Has your faith ever been tested? When you are at the lowest time in your life, and God does a U-turn, how do you handle His test? Hold on to His trust and believe you will make it through. God will put you through many tests, He will guide you in them, and guide you through them. Just keep your mind on Him and follow His will because at the end, it's soul satisfaction. You may not have won the battle, but you've won the war.

I don't think there is a man or woman who has not had bad moments. Even if there is a man or woman who has not been knocked down by life, there will be something that will take you down. God has representatives all over this land. Make no mistake, kindness represents opportunity. Watch what you say to people, you just might be entertaining an angel. Trust your instinct, there is no greater joy than going about God's business. Stay encouraged, lay the foundation, mark your territory, God is always watching. Wake up every morning with a strong will to do something extraordinary for someone.

Whatever follows the words "I AM" will determine what you want in your life. Nothing good happens on earth without someone praying. You have to be strong against Satan, he too has representatives walking around trying to get you into his kingdom (the pit of hell). We should maintain victory in our lives so that Satan will not move us left or right. The enemy wants to kill you but maintain your confidence knowing who you are in the Lord and stand in your strength to keep your faith foremost and steadfast.

FAITH WILL LEAD YOU ON

As Christians, we need to stand on the Word of God. Everybody has an evil day, but always stand on the righteousness of God; put on the whole armor of God. When you are stressed you are hindering the Holy Ghost from performing in your life. Everything has been given to you by God, take it and use it to stabilize your mind and your growth in Him.

When you are born again, you receive the Holy Spirit. It's up to you to take another step in allowing God to use you for His purpose. There are certain things in your life that God will shift for the next twenty years. God changes the way the justice system looks at DNA. The world is changing your perception of everything. Look at your life, has it not changed from one century to another. Even day by day our lives begin to change whether it's positive or negative. Our world takes on a new life – your body, your thoughts, and your outlook on life. You ask yourself if you should stay on the same road and call it a safe haven or if you should challenge the unknown. Strong faith will take you where your desires lie.

Don't take that leap of faith if you are not ready to jump because things will shift. You have to be ready to perform the no return method. Be ready to hold on to God's unchanging hands. The road is about to become bumpy. Don't let anything derail you from keeping your promise to God. God will always have His eyes on you.

■   ■   ■

Chapter 17

Celebrate Your Victory

M y sisters and brothers, don't dampen your desire to dance. If God has given you joy and peace, celebrate with Him. If you want to be loved and adored, you must be able to celebrate God. If you fail to appreciate what God has given you, what you may see coming in, you may later see walking out, because you haven't known how to receive God's wealth.

Take coverage, God's people, please don't be intimidated by those around you. Don't allow subservient positions or poor wages to stifle your lips of praise. Be renewed in your mind, you are in the right place at the right time. God will use you as only He can. Listen carefully, the master conductor is about to give you your cue. Amazing, isn't it, that God can know you're a loose person and still offer a candle to light your way from the darkness of the night into the brightness of the light? He is saying, "Beloved, I want you. I've already paid the price to buy you back. Come home."

Perhaps you are dealing with some issues that seem insurmountable. No matter how badly you are wounded, how sick, how lonely; no matter how many others have pushed past you on the way to the top, keep moving on toward Jesus, the healer. And when He heals you, maybe you should go public and let the world know that an unclean person – a person without a dime in his pocket or a friend to his name, can touch a holy God. Let the world know you made it from disgrace to grace, carried to Him on whispers of hope.

And so my sisters and brothers, I want to tell you that God is a Father who always takes care of His children. You need not be distressed, or walk in fear wondering if the Father will provide. He may not always appear, but He will always provide. For those traumatic moments when everything that you love has been compromised, and all of your hopes have fallen short of reality, you must learn to stand and watch. You may even shed a tear, but you will know that you have given it back to the Father. God will always be your unseen partner. One extraordinary thing we must remember is that life is the creator, we are the performers. If we search deep within ourselves, we will find our spirits wants to know more about the God we serve. I believe we all need a breathing place to wonder and extend the boundaries of ourselves. There is a place out there for each of us. Find it, and you will find yourself.

ENJOY YOUR LIFE

Do you believe that the eyes are the window of the soul? The elderly usually say that the soul reveals life's pressures. Faith has to come when you release yourself to God, giving Him your all.

I challenge every person to resist the temptation to live in a vacuum. If your broken past has left you suspicious of another as a whole, remember that wholeness will enable you to love the imperfect. To expect to find an ideal person, one who can be trusted and does not disappoint is neither true nor realistic. Nor is it true that if you demand such a person, that you yourself could live up to those standards. It is a trick the enemy uses to stop you from enjoying your life, it is a lofty expectation that is fictitious and non-existent. People do fail – men, women, and children fail. But thanks be to God. He does not fail! He loves you in spite of what He knows about you. The real challenge is to receive His love and learn to become secure enough to emulate that love in your relationship. Without that, you will have tremendous standards but absolutely no companionship. The walls that you build to protect yourself will actually imprison you, and time will escape like sand trickling through an hourglass. If you have spent all your life in promiscuity, have suffered from low self-esteem, or are so starved for attention that you will accept it by the hour, the night or the weekend, you need to know that a real relationship with God will heal the void. Then when you are ready to enter into a relationship, it will be for the right reason and not because of that insatiable thirsting for affirmation that causes your relationships to be destroyed. Be the best you can be for God. Because no matter what your past is, your future is still spotless. Remember, your house is not clean if your closet is still dirty. You cannot do God's will without God. The greatest success is to humble yourself and serve others.

LIVE YOUR BEST LIFE

Hell has no fear like a woman in power. Every attempt to move to faith will be met with opposition. Every hater has a purpose to overturn your faith. You have to use your every method of authority to keep your heart and mind occupied with the Word of God. Satan knows stress and anger will destroy you, but you should know, you are super human! God called the end, the beginning so, don't panic when you see the end. You have the gift from God to conquer any battle that is put in front of you. Deliverance and healing are already there. God is your eternal and loving Savior. Be led by grace. Live your best life. God chose you to carry out His vision.

Be part of a world change and look for ways to help others. Be an active supporter and remember grace and peace are the keys to happiness. It's God's way of showering you with His love. Don't be led by your feelings, follow Jesus and fit into God's purpose. God will give you the role He wants you to fit in.

Each day brings a different concept, there's a new season coming your way. There is a resource that will take you to the next level. Let God do it. It will happen. Take your hands off of it because it will take you years or you may never accomplish having your peace and joy. My mother used to say: "It's not my will, it's God and God alone." Don't get crammed in a place where you don't fit. You want to do what you were created to do.

When you wake up each morning, who knows what God will show you. Sometimes, you don't see the reverence in your life. God is reverence, you release faith with your mouth. This is your day and this is your heavenly Father's world. He created it just for you, you are the heir to the universe. Your only boundaries are your own perceptions of potential.

You can reach farther than your fingers and leap higher than your doubts. If you lift your head and raise your hands, the clouds will run away. Surely you have been kissed by the raven sun. Didn't you know that? Haven't you realized that's the reason you are alive? So go on – show up and show off! It's your time to live. It's your morning.

YOU'RE MOVING ON UP

Tell the executives to make room for black pumps and tweed suits. You are moving from the poor house to the White House. Fresh out of fear, God's women are on the move. Real spiritual advantage does not come from the color of your skin. It's not the color that brings deliverance and help from God; it's the contents of your heart. Some of us have certain problems because of where we came from. You may say, "My people came over on a boat and picked cotton on a plantation." But God says that "there is neither Greek nor Jew." He says that there is no such thing as a black church or a white church. There is only one church, purchased by the blood of the lamb. We are all one in Christ Jesus.

Faith is the only thing in this world that gives truly equal opportunity. God looks at the faith that lives within our hearts.

Your treasure is powerful in God's services and the devil knows it. What he doesn't know is that your treasure is also a weapon you can use to defeat him in your life. The devil will do anything he can to sabotage your self-esteem. He doesn't want you developing your assets because he doesn't want you to give birth to what God has put within you. So get ready people of the living God and soon you'll hold a treasure in your arms.

We are all students now in the school of life. Heaven is giving out diplomas, you will learn about life. The discerning person learns wisdom from the idiot and folly from the intelligent, you must have the perception to look deeply into life and then apply what you see. You will see that every incident, every feeling, every fear is a class.

I encourage you to learn all that you can. At the same time, understand that you must learn from others without losing the core of who you are. Your essence may be cultivated but do not allow anyone to mutilate the person you were created to be. Don't get lost in the maze of life and end up being something different from what you were designed to be.

YOU ARE A CHILD OF THE KING

You are a person of the King! In short, whatever you need – natural or spiritual, God is the source from which your blessings must come. You will not look to men. Blessings may come through men but not from them. All of your help will come from the Lord. He will use people from time to time, but your deepest needs, He will fill Himself. He alone can give the soul release. Man sets bones, but God causes them to knit together. Man gives love, but God fills voids. Whatever the arena, remember to include Him.

Do not join the masses of women and men who are chasing after the affections of some fictional lover whose shiny armor is a mere fantasy that will never be humanly realized. Don't become bitter as you rummage through relationships looking for divine love from human hearts. Don't fall into the trap of thinking that there is somewhere beneath the sun's bright light, a hero who isn't tarnished with human flaws. If you are to love a man, understand that he is a man, you will never be disappointed by what you don't expect. The basis of any relationship must be trust, trusting God with your successes isn't much of a challenge. The real test of trust is sharing your secrets, your inner failures and fears. Once you realize this, all your attempts at silence and secrecy will seem childish and ridiculous. He is "the all-seeing ONE," and He knows perfectly and completely what is in you. When you pray, and more importantly, when you commune with God, you must have the kind of confidence and assurance that neither requires nor allows deceit.

God loves me and His love is incomprehensible, primarily because there is nothing with which to compare it. God does not change; neither does His compassion. One thing we search for at every level of our relationships is to be understood, I don't always have to express and explain. Thank you, Lord, for not asking me to explain what I can scarcely express! You have nothing to fear – your honesty with the father won't reveal anything He doesn't already know. His intellect is so keen that He doesn't have to wait for you to make a mistake. He knows about your failure before you fail. His knowledge is all inclusive, spanning the gap between time and incident. He knows your thoughts even as you subconsciously gather them in your own mind.

Jesus once told the woman at the well:

> True worshipers will worship the Father in spirit and truth; for the Father is seeking people to worship Him. God is a spirit, and those who worship Him must worship in spirit and truth. (John 4:23-24)

Sometimes, your anointing is not at the appointed time. But wait – you don't get to abruptly go back to the cubicle and wait because God is humbling you. It's not yet your time, God always does things in the fullness of time. Go on and shout about it. "It's coming!" When you move into a new level, remember that it comes with more conflict and hard work. Will you be able to handle your promotion? If you associate success with prayer, you will need God to be aboard. People will follow you if you inspire them. Choose your battles carefully, lead and not follow. Remember, the devil will always return no matter what. The Bible says you are never, ever too late to have faith in God.

"Lord, I'm an independent spirit. I've been on my own, made my own choices, and I take care of myself. At times, submission comes easily, but not right now. You have placed authority in my life as a means of protection, not as a means of control. I don't want to be like the stiff-necked people in the Bible, so I need your help. I ask you to give me supernatural wisdom so that I will make godly decisions. I ask you to fill my life with love so that I will be glad to submit to those whom you have chosen for me. Make me so full of your spirit that I cannot help but respect my fellow man. Help me, Lord, to crucify the flesh in me that tries to rebel. Cleanse me of every rebellious thought. Keep me from confusing your definition of submission with the world's definition. Thank you for bringing me to an understanding of true, holy submission and servanthood."

BE YOURSELF

Now there are lots of people whom I admire. I may admire some of their attributes or think they look wonderful or appreciate the way they do certain things. But I have never met anyone who had anything about them that I found so wonderful or so intimidating that I was willing to give up being me in order to try to be them. NO WAY!

You must be able to say to another person: "You don't approve of me? You don't like the way I look? You don't like the way I talk? You don't think I'm a qualified person? You don't think

I have value? You don't think I'm worthy? You don't think I have purpose and reason for being that are just as important as that of the next person?" I disagree! You don't have to get mad about it to prove that you're right and they're wrong, you simply disagree. You take the position and just before you walk away, you simply and calmly say, you have your opinion, but I also have mine. You know God values you, now, it is time to look yourself and others in the eye and say: "Excuse me, but I have the right to express myself and have my opinions. I choose to agree with what God says about me!"

OPEN AND CLOSED DOORS

You know you're up against a shut door when it will not open. I know this seems obvious because we often have to pray to get a door open when the enemy is trying to discourage us. Here's a simple way to tell the difference: if the door is just closed by the enemy, and he is trying to get you to give up on your dream, prayer and praise will unlock it. But if the door is closed by a sovereign decision of the all-wise God, and prayer and praise do not open it, then you must accept His decision.

But I want to take this a step further. We can readily accept His authority when it is used to perform what we know to be a favor. The real challenge of submission is to submit when your human will wants to choose another way. This is the graduation exercise of faith and the commencement service of a trust for those whose dependence and reliance is upon the manifold wisdom of God. Never underestimate the power of a shut door!

Many of us have been through so much that we exist like empty houses on crowded streets. We are standing amid the activities of life, but there is no light in us. Some may not notice, but a discerning eye cannot help but see the evidence of a deserted heart and a forsaken smile. Some of us have lost the iridescent shimmer that suggests life. We have stopped life making. We are just holding on. We have fallen into the lethargy of those who aren't expecting company. But God says, "Arise and know in your heart that Jesus is coming." But God didn't stop there. He also promised that Abraham's seed would be as the stars of heaven. We too are seeds of Abraham. Whatever God gives you, He wants it to multiple in your spirit. When you bring it forth, it shall be greater than what you had. The enemy wants to put multiple fears in your life. God wants to set you free from fear and fill you with faith, you must trust Him enough to allow Him to come in and plow up your life. He may need to root out closet skeletons and replace them with new attitudes.

Satan wants to block you and cause less productivity. Don't be afraid. You are one of God's people.

> Delight thyself also in the LORD: and he shall give thee the desires of thine heart. (Psalm 37:4)

God has promised to give you the desires of your heart. He always keeps His promises! Look to God when there are needs in your life. He satisfies like calm sheep grazing in the afternoon sun, you will find fulfillment for your soul and contentment with yourself.

CELEBRATE THE TREASURE IN YOU

Every person alive is a treasure chest. Each one holds something God intends for you to use in fulfilling His purpose for your life. And in the process, you will bring Him glory. Find out what treasure God has hidden in you because the devil is going to fight you for it. He knows the treasure is there, and he wants it for his purpose. He wants it badly. So many people today are fighting the Devil and don't even know why. It's because they haven't discovered the treasure that lies within them. The Devil knows it's there. God knows it's there. So the fight is on.

When the devil gets a hold of your life, he will wreck your very soul. What's pushing you over the edge? You are not fighting against a devil that's not organized. He will attack children who are still in diapers. He will mold them to serve him. When God is not in your life, the fight is on winning your children and showing them that drugs and gangs are mischiefs meant to bring you and your family down to the pit of no return. But when God steps in – no weapon formed against you shall prosper.

Talk to the devil, tell him, he can run up on your family if he wants to, but he will limp back. Push for your family, pray for your family, fight for your family. Tell the devil, let the door hit you where the good Lord split you. Take charge of your house!

We serve a God who is sovereign, loving, giving, and loves us with all that He has. God looked out across eternity. He saw everything He had created and everything He would create around you. He saw the full set of traits and abilities that you would need in order to complete His purpose for your life. He knew what kind of environment would be necessary for you to properly develop the gifts He would give you. Do you have the same opinion of yourself? In order for people to treat you well, there must be something deep inside of you that sends out a signal saying, "I am somebody" because God made me to be somebody. I may not be twenty-one and wear a size seven, but I am somebody. When you send out a signal like that, other people pick up on it.

There is something your spirit exudes that gives you presence with others. There's a quality of inner strength that makes you attractive. It causes other people to recognize you, to pay attention to you, to ask when you walk into a room, "who is she?" They won't be asking because your dress is so stunning, but because your character is so magnetic; projecting that kind of strength is not arrogance or pride. It is healthy self-esteem and the power of God's spirit within you.

APPRECIATE GOD'S CREATION
The way you appreciate yourself impacts on everything you do. It affects the way you sit in a classroom, apply for a job, talk to people at a social function, or go about the ministry God has called you to undertake. It even affects the way you pray and the way you study God's Word.

God wants you to appreciate who He made you to be and develop what He gave you. You are a unique blend of talents, gifting and character – you have a unique destiny upon this earth. You are somebody!

When you have a problem, most people will call you the crack head or whatever the demon has over you. When Satan gets a hold of you, you become uncontrollable, you are now bound with chains. Satan will shut you up and attack you with everything he has. Watch out for demons in suits and fine dresses. They are out to destroy you. To wreck your homes, destroy your family and turn your life upside down. Be aware, travel the waters highly, don't let the devil bring you to your knees.

You are not outnumbered if you trust and let God lead you. Allow God to be your G.P.S. Your enemy already knows you are coming. Your destiny is unstoppable. God has inspired you to lead others to His kingdom. Your life is not a destination, it's a journey. It's as simple as putting one foot in front of the other and making every step count for something positive. God wants us to listen to our minds but follow our hearts. There is peace and contentment in the Word of God.

Do you know how powerful you are? When you get a phone call in the middle of the night, and you don't blink an uncertain eye at the time, you know the devil cannot move you? That's how great and reliable my God is. Give Him the praise, trust Him. He is worthy to be praised. Can you lean on Him? Yes! Yes! You can.

Discouragement will ride with you going to work and pick-up when going home. When you see struggles approaching, keep walking, keep praying because your steps are ordered by God. Before I retired, I wanted to leave the workforce, but God showed me it was not the right time. Because I had not taken the steps He had prepared for me. Make no mistake, there are roads you will have to walk and mountains you will have to climb before pleasing God. God will not crown you until the job is done. Stay on track with the Word of God – you will get there. Don't complain, don't murmur, and don't get off course. You will reach the place God has for you.

CHALLENGE YOURSELF

Keep an even temper, study what is important to God. Walk in the fruit of joy because this is not your world. After all, God said you are worth fighting for. Nothing can separate you from God's love.

Keep moving, keep fighting, and keep praying. It's your time to shine. Eyes have not seen, ears have not heard, all God has planned for you. There is so much more worth fighting for. When God is in the building, it does not matter if it's raining or the sun is shining, your faith should always be solid as a rock. When you get to a period in your life to take a breather, sit back and look at where or how far you have come. Then keep it moving. It's not the steps you leave behind that matters. It's the steps you take moving forward that will frame your future. What will give you purpose is in your grasp.

Make sure you break your pattern; your pattern keeps you in a prison. It's good to have fear, it's not good for fear to have you. Step into an unfamiliar world, challenge yourself. Your destiny may be waiting.

Do you associate yourself with money or prayer? Do you know you are in the middle of a transition? Make no mistake, you are anointed to do what God wants you to do. God recognizes your vulnerability about being a receptacle. By nature, women are wide open, but men are closed. You must be careful what you allow to plug into you and draw strength from you. The wrong plug can drain your power.

Eve allowed herself to be uncovered by Satan who plugged into her desire to see, taste, and be wise. The enemy took advantage of her weaknesses. Be careful who you let uncover you. The wrong person can lead you to complete destruction. Be on guard, if the Devil can get you to help meet his purpose, you will belong to him and not to God. Your prayer time needs to increase to an all-time high. When you begin to put things in priority, people will begin to hate you. Don't detour. God values you because you are the apple of His eyes. God loves you! When your past does not show up in your future – that is the time when you know you are the righteousness of God. Do not live in bitterness, don't stay in pain, don't let anyone take you there. God's priority is loving you. Faith works when you believe how much God loves you. God's everlasting love will always outweigh any situation that will come upon you. Stay hungry for the Word of God.

You may not have an abundance of education but just remember, God always uses the people who have the least.

God has the power to make you a victorious person. God has a way of conquering all your problems. God always has a miracle in store for you. Do you realize God is in charge of your life? The devil cannot make a move on you unless you give Him the power to do so? Let God break down those barriers so you can seek God's face without fear. Use your faith, so God can use your heart and mind.

■ ■ ■

Chapter 18

God's Purpose Must Prevail

On Thanksgiving 2015, my sciatic nerve hurt so severely, I began walking like a two-year-old. I tried every pain medication I could think of for seven days. I prayed and prayed. I said to God: "I've done all I know how to do. I'm putting my illness in your capable hands." On the eighth day, I began to feel a little better. Each day was better than the day before. By the tenth day, I was cleaning my house and preparing a meal for myself. I was back in full swing. That's the power of God's mercy. All I relied on were the promises of God and the love of God. He brought greatness out of an unhealthy situation. Bad never looks as bad when God's hands are all over it. Hold onto God's Word and let it wrap around your heart.

Sometimes, your circumstances will take you where your spiritual life doesn't want to go. Value your anointing, God will deliver you from all your uncertainties. It's time to get yourself together, you are standing on fresh oil. Satan loves to deal with people who are isolated. In your mind, you will wonder, "What is wrong with me?" Your thoughts will take you in a direction of inferiority, Satan will send somebody to confuse you because you feel so alone. Don't give in, you don't need anyone to mess up your life. Sometimes, you would rather be alone. Don't allow Satan and his gang to destroy your peace. God knows how to put together what you long for. God already has your gift. But are you ready for it? Don't trip, you can do it. Remember, the world has its privileges.

Have you ever looked for God in your situation and couldn't find Him? What do you do? Make sure your heart is in the will of God. God said touch not my anointed. Your problems are not greater than the power of God over you. God will walk your problems straight out of your life. Because weeping may endure for a night, but joy comes in the morning. When your hand is in God's hands, your blessings will chase you down. Your cup will run over, peace will knock at your door, joy will unlock any door, and the love of God will grant you eternal serenity.

A MIRACLE WORKING GOD

I know that Jesus is alive today because miracles still happen. Just put all your faith in the hands of the Almighty, and He will see you through. God will bring things to life that you thought were dead. God is the giver of life, He parted the Red Sea, He made all things possible. Don't struggle with small things, you are a child of the Most High, looking to fulfill your destiny. God will do what you cannot do.

One night, I was listening to Joel Osteen. His sermon was "The Great I Am." As I look back at my life, I realize the great "I am" was always with me – carrying me, walking with me, moving mountains, pushing aside stumbling blocks, talking to me, and opening doors for me. And now, I have seen it all come together like the pages of a book folding together.

All by the hand of the Almighty. I am so grateful God pushed me to be the best I can possibly be. Now, I know my life is in God's hand to do His will. I know I'm in a positive and relentless world of peace. God knew exactly what I needed.

God has already exposed you to the truth. You cannot go backward. You have to get out of the prison you built. You cannot stay there with the morals of your past life. Change has to come if you want a better life.

Birthing a new life is traumatic, it's a separation of self-habits. It requires pushing, shelving, and praying. You have to remain calm, it's going to take a lot more than you anticipated. Go on and take it to the next level. When doors close, don't give up. God's ears and eyes are still on you. Your opportunity has already been birthed. This is not the time to become tired because weakness always brings the devil in faster. Take a stand, the Lord will be your crutch. Get to a place where you hold a high opinion of yourself based on the fact that God made you exactly, precisely, intricately, wondrously, and uniquely. You are a one-of-a-kind creation for which there is no comparison.

God made you for His own purposes so that you might reflect a unique aspect of His glory. When you cease to compare yourself with others and refuse to be intimidated by what other people think and say, you are then in the position to birth that business, that ministry, that effort to change your community that God intended. How dare you compare yourself with somebody? God wanted you to be you. NO ONE ELSE!

GOD MAKES NO MISTAKES

Don't challenge God by telling Him that He made a mistake, He failed and you could have done a better job creating you.

None of us has the privilege of criticizing God. He is the Creator who looks at each of His created beings and says to Himself, "It is good." God is the God of vision, He also is the God of provision. God has given us everything we need. Use your faith for something big. God has enormous shoulders and if you put your faith and trust in Him, your road will be paved with gold. Don't try to purchase God with funds because that never works, your faith will carry you further than anything you can possibly imagine. God's grace will make you a winner if you just trust Him. He will undoubtedly show up and show off. All goodness and happiness come from God! Be careful how you manage God's belongings. Do you know you belong to Him? You are not that important to claim credit for God's work. Let God be the source of your provision.

When burdens overpower your world and put you in a state of despair, will you trust Him? When your life becomes so complicated and bombarded with troubles and your children are out of control – what do you do? What do you do when nothing seems to pull together?

Don't sit there and act like your life is and has always been perfect. There is a demonic spirit floating around you. How do you get back your peace and joy that have disappeared? Rise above your problem and trust God with His goodness; remember, you are highly favored – God has not left you. Don't run away from Him, run toward Him because He is always waiting.

A problem is like a snowball waiting for a target. No matter what the problem may be, you were put there to fight the fight and win. Agony may set in, but you have to ride it until wrong turns to right; weeping may come but joy will come on time. If you just hold on, God will restore all you have lost. Be patient, right now, you may be in the middle of a storm. You may be afraid but don't step backward, your blessings are just an inch away. God knows what's going on in your life, stay encouraged, keep on walking and do not faint, you will live! That's the power of the Almighty.

OPPOSITION OR OPPORTUNITY?

Do you realize the same way you came into this world naked and clueless, is the same way you will leave this world? God wants us to be covered like an outlet is covered, in order that no one tampers with its intended purpose. Be on guard.

How many people did you start out with? Now look around you – who is standing with you? Nobody but God. Trust only God to show you the life you want to live. God chose you for the fight, that's why you are still standing. Get fit for the fight. Put on the whole armor because you will need a shield to protect you from the stones that are coming at you. Continue to live the life God has prepared for you. Your mountains will become stepping stones; your burdens will only stay for a moment. Your future will become brighter. God will strengthen your heart, and you will sustain all that comes at you. God will be your guard over troubled waters.

Your opposition may be your opportunity to go after your destiny. You have to get off your behind and make that move. Don't announce everything to people, you may be stifling your blessings. But God can hide things in front of you, and they will not be revealed until God is ready. How many times have you slid by through turmoil and hard situations without being bruised or tampered with? God hides things in you.

Look deep within yourself and allow God to continue to hide the precious gifts in you until He is ready to challenge your mind to fulfill your destiny. Whatever stage you stand on, there will always be haters, those who say you will be nothing, your opportunity is your opposition. Whatever you focus on, you will strengthen.

Perhaps, you have been haunted by one of these issues or some other crisis. Have you known what it was like to want someone to rescue you from pain? Well, my people, let me save you some precious time. Only the Lord can heal deep pain. It does not matter whether your pain comes from a brutal rape, kept secrets, fractured promises or some other gut-wrenching disturbance. He is the Prince of Peace, and He rides into the worst situations on the wings of hope. His divine hand over you gives sense to the tragic events that seemed meaningless. He knows how to orchestrate your pain and somehow bring a blessing out of a mess.

Reach out and embrace the fact that God has been watching over you all your life. My sister, brother, He covers you, clothes you, and blesses you. Rejoice in Him in spite of the broken places. God's grace is sufficient for your needs and your scars and so, it should be when we look at our lives. God has put us together in a way that cannot and should not be replicated. He chose every aspect of our personalities, crafted every gift and talent that He bestowed on us and gave special thought to each one of our features and traits – we were handmade by Him. He custom-designed us to fit a specific role in His sovereign plan. Nobody has ever been just like you, and nobody ever will be just like you. You are a designer original – have you ever celebrated yourself? Have you ever praised God for the way He made you? If not, today is a good day to begin.

I remember working for the Baltimore Infant and Toddlers Program. I arrived early to get my workload down to a minimum. As I was coming from the resource area, there was a young man walking towards me with an arm full of toys. I asked him: "What are you doing in here? He brushed past me to get on the elevator. When the door opened, I proceeded to follow him. He pushed me, I stumbled backward and the door closed. Of course, the police were called and the director was informed.

As the day went on, I began to think what would have happened if I had gotten on the elevator with this person. God has His way of blocking situations that are not conducive to His plan. The situation could have been much worse. I thank God for His mercy and protection.

WAVE YOUR PAIN GOODBYE

Sometimes, you have to tell people, "My middle name is *possible* and my last name is *succeed*." You should like what you stand for. Keep your hands on the future and wave goodbye to the pain of the past. All your actions have consequences. You should have gifts and the ability to say you like yourself.

Ladies, if you are not selling it, don't post it. Keep yourself for the permanent one. God will bring your request to pass. People, never ever get to the point where nobody can tell you anything. Always be willing to expand your knowledge. Nobody sinks but the dumb and the ignorant. Pull yourself together and let God lead you into the best promotions. Reach back and pull your fellow man with you. God is watching how you handle your faith. Don't let God down. Pass the test.

Somehow, on your journey, you will cross the roads of uncertainty. Will you remain stuck or will you pray your way out?

Be a student in God's class. You are not defined by your past, you are prepared by your past. Get rid of that baggage. It's too heavy, you need not carry it. There is too much out there to be joyous about. Nothing is a surprise to God, He knows everybody who will hurt you, and God will be your vindicator. Talk to God, don't live bitter – live better. Focus on all God has for you, your past is not your future. Forget what lies behind, let go of that negative energy. Don't talk about, don't think about, bury it, have a funeral for it. It's your past.

Don't push people away with your stinky ways. Sometimes, when we stink, we don't realize it. Bad attitudes and poor dispositions will defeat you and smell up your life. Drop them, leave them, and let them go. God will fight your battles. Don't keep picking up your problems, put a sign on them, and label them destroyed. God wants to do something new in your life, but you have to drop your problems and give God the right away. God doesn't thrive on moments. Moments come and go, you want a good and permanent lifestyle. You will come into an abundance of more than enough.

We have to remember and realize that our bodies are just the shells of who we are. They are just containers for our humanness.

Don't leave this world with questions. Push a little harder toward your goals. Don't let that little voice sit on your shoulders and talk you out of your gifts. Don't let fear hold you back. You have to believe God is there to act positively on your behalf. You cannot be successful being afraid. Accomplish what you were called to do because you are on a divine mission for God. You may have to crawl to get there, but keep crawling. You may have to cry a lot of tears along the way, but keep walking. You may get knocked down, but get up and get going. Don't let anything keep you from your mission. The thing that God has for you must be done. You must keep your mission in front you. Obedience is the key to being successful. It must be kept!

Thousands of people are afraid but the church can give strength to counter that fear. Thousands have built walls around themselves because they don't trust anyone else. The body of Christ can help its members regain trust.

Thousands more are codependent and get value from a relationship with another person. The church can point to God's love as the source of self-worth. We are not valuable because we love God; we are valuable because He loves us.

One of the main reasons people don't share their problems is this; they are told they shouldn't have problems especially after they are saved! In Hebrews 11, we find a list of people who are often called the heroes of faith. On the list, you'll see Noah and Abraham, Sarah, Moses, Rahab, Gideon, David, Samuel and all the prophets. The amazing thing is that every one of these giants of faith had a problem. God's people have problems. We need to face up to that. It's not a matter of lack of faith or not being saved. It's a fact of life in a fallen world. Problems come with the turf of a world that has been turned upside down by sin. For the wounded and hurting, God has intensive care units. There may be times in your life when God nurtures you through a crisis. On the other hand, you may not even realize the many times He intervenes to relieve the tensions and stresses of everyday living.

SAFE IN JESUS' ARMS

God knows when the load is overwhelming, and He moves just in the nick of time. The Lord Himself gives us new days. He sees us through all stormy times; they will cease and when they pass, we will be safe in the arms of our Lord, the Master of all seasons.

Don't focus on things that will hurt you. Don't give strength to your weaknesses. Some people focus on getting rich, and completely ignore God. You will not gain favor from God using your own methods. Every good and perfect gift comes from God. We should rely, depend and lean on God. We are not the source of our lives; God is. The next step of greatness is closer than you believe. Do not critique what's wrong and ignore what's right. You may be saved now, but you need to look into the Lord's way of life and embrace the opportunity to go the exact mile. Don't delay your transition. Life has a lot to offer you. Life is bigger than your dreams. God has a plan for you. It's a divine plan.

Be comfortable with leaving behind what you cannot take with you. Don't rest on what you have already accomplished, always challenge yourself to more. Keep a vision to push forward.

You will never give birth to your future if you keep looking back. Remain loyal to your future, each day with God brings better choices and accomplishments. Be aware of favors, God's favors are to bless and profit you. The devil's favors are to trick, destroy, and humiliate you. Never let the lack of faith keep you from the promises God has for you. God wants you to know above all else, He loves you.

If your true desire is to be happy, tell Jesus to take the wheel. It's easy to complain, Jesus knows how you feel. It's time to take the rear view mirror off because Jesus will bless you when it's time. If you are in turmoil on the inside, it will show on the outside. If you need God's power to get over adversities call Him on the main line. That's your hook-up for mercy and glory.

Don't trade in your peace for anyone. People come and go, but God is stable. Everybody has a pattern and the devil will use your pattern against you. You can run around the church, dance down to your knee caps, yell, wave your hands, and still have no peace. That's when you have to pray harder and move the devil out. Take your peace back, don't let the devil think he has won. This is the time to repent and move to a higher level in your faith. Trust me, the peace of the world is based on what is going on around you. God wants to give you comfort and peace. Listen to the melodies of your soul because they will give you serenity and recharge your mind. God has placed a plan in you that no one can destroy. Please stop worrying, you are never without God. When you worry, you create sin. Because God can fix anything if only you will allow Him to. Get out of God's way! Look back over your life – hasn't He given you peace in the middle of storms? Trust God! If you don't, the devil will bring humiliation and havoc in your way without a blink. Don't become weak! The reality is, if you are not strong, the devil will plan your life and try to hinder you with road blocks, stumbling blocks, death, and many more obstacles. Please don't run from God, run as fast as you can to Him. He loves taking care of you.

Listen to me – the devil is no match for God. When you declare favor over your life, there's nothing the devil can do because God has you in the palm of His hands, guiding you, preparing you, and keeping you above all the negatives that are coming toward you. If you want to know what your life will be like five years from now, listen to what you speak over your life. We all are going to die, but don't speak your way on a downward spiral. In spite of what you feel, declare favor over your body and speak health over your life. Don't talk about the way you are, instead, talk about how you want your future to be. God promises beauty for ashes. Move away from self- pity. Take a few moment and write down how you want your life to be. You have royal blood in your veins, move toward a rewarding and prosperous life.

GOD'S HAS GREAT PLANS FOR US

Too often, we settle for less than God wants for us. You may be satisfied, but God is not. He will open doors that will amaze you. You will always encounter great blessings when you embrace God's second touch. God is the Author and the Finisher of our faith. When you go through disappointments, look for a shift in your soul – that's God working out your problems. God has planted a seed in you, He will water it if you allow Him. God will lift you out of your pit; He will not give up on you. God knew there will be times when you get tired. He is a rescuer; He has millions of anointed servers to help you on your journey. God will never disqualify you for making a mistake.

Don't stay in a painful situation, don't let bad breaks or uncertainties discourage you. The enemy cannot stop God's plan for your life. Stop hanging on by a thread, save yourself from anger and despair. God said it's over, trust Him. See yourself clearly, the road is wide open, walk that extra mile because God is always waiting.

God has always amazed me with His glorious gifts. His love will launch you into a new level of life. Don't settle where you are. Stir your faith and start believing and serving God. It's your season, let Him move in.

Love is a leap of faith, sometimes, you just have to jump. Asking God for help is not a sign of weakness, it's a sign of strength. God will get you where you want to go, but it's up to you to persevere. It's opposition or opportunity, which will you choose? God has everything working for your good, and He did it intentionally; He has spoken, let the people say, amen.

WE ARE GOD'S HEART BEAT

Pick up your baggage and toss it into the sea of forgetfulness. Your bad times have turned into good times. If the devil tries to take your mind, plead war. He can only take what you allow him to take. God knows you are worth saving, He gave us hope, and He changed my life; I will praise Him forever. There were sacrifices made so I could be free. I know everything will be alright. So dry all tears and get on board, the glory train is about to take off. God's love is strong and His heart is pure. He sees everything, the battle is not yours, it's the Lord's.

This country thrives on words. We all know hate is a powerful word, but love is stronger. You can always shoot for the moon even if you miss, you will be among the stars. I know I stand on the shoulders of giants. My God has instilled in me love and caring for my fellow man. "No," I could not have made it without God and the people who have fought and slaved to make this world what it is today, God has made us recognize the greatness He put in us. I thank God for allowing me to raise my voice and express the knowledge I have endured from my ancestors. I do not take my life lightly, it's a trial and error to make each day the most glorious day ever. At the end of each day, my sincere life and loyalty belong to God and God alone.

Life is about giving praise where praise is due. When there is no love, there is little joy and peace.

In the late sixties, I remember going downtown Baltimore to Hecht's, Stewarts, Hoch's companies. The moment we stepped into the establishment, we were followed and we were not allowed to try on clothing because of the color of our skin. Blacks were followed throughout the stores. Our civil rights leaders changed the way we were addressed and treated. People respect leaders such as Dr. Martin Luther King, Jr., Julian Bond, Shirley Chisholm and the NAACP. They followed God's lead and brought us out of bondage.

I look at some of our children today who are fighting for freedom and some are fighting to stay out of jail. Our voices have to keep instilling values, morals, and principles that are so needed in our children. Our children are our followers; they are watching us with a watchful eye. We have to encourage them because we are their greatest cheerleaders. Our Father in heaven will always be at our side. We have to put forth the effort to stand and accept the hand we have chosen.

Don't let stressful situations discourage you. The test you are experiencing shows your belief in the Father. God is very patient. He will give you chances after chances to get your life in order. Ask God for guidance, don't make decisions you'll regret.

Put your hand on your chest and feel the beating of your heart. The rhythm that you feel is steady and consistent. It has a pattern and a direction – so is the Father's love. I want you to know, to feel and to experience deeply a Father's heart! We are the Father's heartbeat, and He loves us so. He will ask you to release and turn from thoughts, actions, and conditions of your heart that are not pleasing to Him. He wants you to live and to abide in purity, humor, honor, and love. Please do not break His heart by living in sin. He has a reason for asking you to give up areas that compromise true holiness. He isn't saying no because He is mean; He is saying no because He wants something better for you than what you have. He is not the kind of God to deny you. He is trying to wrench a little sin out of your hand because He knows it will eventually destroy you, your children or your self-esteem. Let it go!

CONCLUSION

Sometimes, all we need is a change in direction. God can do that. He will send someone to put us on the right trail. Sometimes, we just need to be touched by an angel. Have you ever been pruned by God? When God starts peeling off layers of unacceptable behaviors, you say to yourself, God are you going to leave anything? Look at a plant being pruned, when it starts to grow back, it begins to look healthier and better than before. That's what happens when God wants to prune us. God wants to clear out all unhealthiness and replace it with heavenly instruments. Some of the layers we have are embedded so thick, it will take centuries to peel off all the hate, anxiety, pressures, sadness, hopelessness, blame, selfishness and loneliness, not to mention bad habits.

God has His work cut out for Him. Do yourself a favor, turn it over, only God can make you whole again. Work with God, He will work on you and with you. God takes pleasure in bringing you into a world of pure happiness.

NEVER FORGET GOD'S GRACE

Bishop Dewayne Debnam preached a sermon on November 22, 2015, entitled, "Too Much to Forget." Never forget who brought you through all your battles. He humbled you and sustained you. When God has His hand on your life, you may be bruised but not broken. God has a master plan for you. No doors will close in your face; when we think God is not working, He is working preparing you for your journey. I went through the bad to get to the better. God made me fight, and I overcame it all. The wounds you have suffered got you where God wants you to be. Don't mess up now – be careful, keep going because you are on your way to a breakthrough.

That sermon resonated with me like no other has. I will never forget all God has done in my life.

Never manipulate a moment to mask the present. When you do what God wants, He will fill your life with favor. God has given us the power to endure anything that comes our way. Decide ahead of time, that nothing which comes your way will upset you, God is completely in control; every day is a gift from Him. He has a solution for every problem. There is oil on your life, everything that's not supposed to stick will roll off. Don't be intimidated. No matter what the problem may be, you have the God-given power to defeat any forces of darkness. On the other side of that problem, there is a new destiny. Sometimes, in life, you will feel pushed into areas you cannot defeat, but the solution is to stand back and watch God rescue you. God has given you the opportunity to go get your blessings.

Do not be dismayed, you are on your way to receiving your calling. Your challenge will be your guide to open doors. God placed you there, you are headed to victory. All the forces of darkness cannot stop you. Will you trust Him even though you don't understand? Where you are is not where you are going to stay. There will be manipulation, negativity, and back stabbing put in place but your trust in God will show you the way. Get away from people and their unhealthy ways. Keep moving forward, the breakdowns and upsetting moments are just a test. All your tests are setting you up for a comeback.

Everything works for your good. Stop fighting everything that's not going your way. God creates opportunities to bring you closer to your destiny. Don't live frustrated, come back to that place of great peace. God is greater than anything you can ever imagine. He will strengthen your faith and take you to the places you desire.

God will not allow weakness to reproduce. God will not put His fruit into someone who walks away. Discover who you are. Don't give more to others than you give yourself. What is hiding in you that you have never seen? God's job is to help you identify what you can't see. Allow Him to search your mind, so He can make you the person of greatness. You have what it takes, why don't you use it? Never let your eyes determine what your heart believes. Stop worrying, it's a waste of time. Life is about purpose, not position. Being disobedient can cause blindness to God's vision for you. Turn your worries into battles and learn to trust God more. Let the Master take control of your mind. God has got you. Always look for the obvious. May God bless you.

■   ■   ■

Dedication

Arthur Barnes has always been there to inspire and encourage me to keep writing. He continues to shower me with words of wisdom and integrity. He inspires me to take the world by the tail and give it a run for what it's worth. For this, my beloved, you are one-of-a-kind. You are my love, friend, rock, and companion.

This one is for you!